VATICAN II IN PLAIN ENGLISH

The
Constitutions

VATICAN II IN PLAIN ENGLISH

The Constitutions

by Bill Huebsch

ThomasMore®

Allen, Texas

NIHIL OBSTAT
Rev. Msgr. Glenn D. Gardner, J.C.D.
Censor Librorum
IMPRIMATUR
† Most Rev. Charles V. Grahmann
Bishop of Dallas
November 21, 1996

The Nihil Obstat and Imprimatur are official declarations that the material reviewed is free of doctrinal or moral error. No implication is contained therein that those granting the Nihil Obstat and Imprimatur agree with the contents, opinions, or statements expressed.

ACKNOWLEDGMENT

Scripture quotations are adapted from the New Revised Standard Version of the Bible, copyright 1989 by the Division of Christian Education of the National Council of the Churches of Christ in the USA. Used by permission. All rights reserved.

Send all inquiries to:

Thomas More Publishing
200 East Bethany Drive
Allen, Texas 75002–3804

Printed in the United States of America

Book One	ISBN 0–88347–349–6
Book Two	ISBN 0–88347–350–X
Book Three	ISBN 0–88347–351–8
Slipcase	ISBN 0–88347–348–8

1 2 3 4 5   01 00 99 98 97

CONTENTS

*This book is dedicated
to the memory of
Father Karl Rahner, S.J.*

Introduction

I was digging around one day in a large used book store, one known to have perhaps the largest single collection of used theological books in the world. I was looking for a copy of the documents of Vatican II in Latin.

I had already immersed myself in these documents in their various English translations, mainly the one by Walter Abbott, S.J., and was quite thoroughly familiar with the power and impact of the texts. But I was also aware that for many people in today's Church, these documents are less than fully accessible because of their length and because of the style in which they were composed.

Unless a scholar is in pursuit of some particular point, reading the documents as one would the Psalms, for example, never occurs to us. They aren't as compelling to us as the words of Scripture. And because they are filled with repetition, with long, complicated sentences, and with language carefully chosen to be meaningful to church insiders but not to very many others, they don't stir us deeply even when we do read them!

But I knew they'd been written by bishops from around the world. I knew they'd been hammered out under the guidance of the Holy Spirit, under the leadership of Popes John XXIII and Paul VI, under the hard work of hundreds of theological experts, and under the hope that they would offer the Church much needed reform.

I knew, for example, that Yves Congar had been there. I knew that John Courtney Murray had been there and had practically written the document on religious liberty single-handedly. I knew that Edward Schillebeeckx had been there. Karl Rahner was there, of course. Bernard Häring had been secretary to the commission that drafted the document on the Church in the modern world. I knew that Cardinal Suenens of Belgium had enormous influence, that Cardinal Bea had worked miracles to move the Roman Catholic Church toward ecumenism, that Cardinal Dearden of Detroit had time and again spoken for reform.

I knew of the extraordinary efforts of Maximos Saigh, the colorful and controversial patriarch of the Melchites in the Eastern Church. I had read a speech given by Archbishop Paul Hallinan of Atlanta calling for fuller ministries for women in the Church. I remembered that Cardinals Frings, Alfrink, Lercaro, Dopfner, and Montini had played large roles.

I knew that these people and many other heroes of mine had all spared no effort to assist the council in coming to terms with the modern times and in enacting *aggiornamento* as Pope John XXIII requested.

And I knew that now, some three or more decades after the end of Vatican II, the time had come to return to these valuable modern texts and to approach them with more reverence, with prayer, with reflection, and with each other.

So why, one might ask, was I digging around looking for a Latin edition of them? Well, I was about to begin the project you are now holding, and I had decided that working with the Vatican II documents in their original Latin and consulting various English translations would produce a better paraphrase.

And on that day as I searched in a used book store near my hometown, I found a leather-bound edition of the documents published by the Vatican's own press at the conclusion of the council. Picking it up carefully, I opened the cover and there found the name of John Cardinal Dearden, written in his own hand! How had this copy fallen into public hands after belonging to him?

Working with his own Latin text beside me throughout this project has been almost like having the spirit of Cardinal Dearden here with me as well. And with him, the spirit of all those others. I hold his copy of the documents now as I would a copy of Scripture, knowing that the paragraphs and pages of Cardinal Dearden's book contain the "word of the Church."

Format

I have chosen to present these paraphrases in sense lines to make them more readable for the average user. Written this way, they resemble other spiritual writings, and you can more easily use them for prayer and reflection.

These sense lines are meant to stimulate midrash. This method of coming to grips with and internalizing spiritual writing asks a reader to consider the texts thoroughly and then to offer her or his own reflection on them. In so doing, one "owns" the texts and finds one's own words to explain them to others.

Paul Thurmes, another theologian, worked closely with me in preparing three of the documents in this volume and one in the next. Throughout our work, we faithfully retained the article numbers as they appear in the original texts. Sometimes, however, to make the material flow well, we reorganized certain articles or borrowed from one article to add a complement to another. You should, however, be able to return to a place in any properly numbered text that corresponds exactly to our numbering.

Paul and I remained as faithful to the text as we could be; we put aside our own biases. We did midrash with each other as we proceeded, sometimes late into the night, arguing this verb or that in Latin or Italian, other times seeking answers to translation quandaries by consulting other portions of the document in which we were working or by consulting other council documents that elaborated a particular point more fully.

All in all, we see the three volumes in this series as a way for more Catholics, Jews, other Christians, and all of goodwill to come to understand the writings of the Second Vatican Council and, having understood them better, to join the worldwide campaign to implement them fully and, in so doing, to help establish human solidarity and divine presence in our day.

The Dogmatic Constitution on the Church

Lumen Gentium

Chapter One

PART ONE: BACKGROUND

*I*n a sense, the discussion on the nature of the Church, which *Lumen Gentium* now summarizes, began at Vatican I in the nineteenth century. In preparation for that council, a somewhat lengthy draft document on the Church was prepared. But two factors intervened to prevent a full discussion about the Church from occurring at that time. First, Vatican I was ended abruptly because of wars in Europe. The attending bishops hurried to their home dioceses to avoid armies fighting there as well as a national army advancing on the city of Rome. Second, a conservative movement within the Church at that time, with the support of Pope Pius IX, sought and got a firm definition of papal primacy and infallibility at Vatican I.

The original intention of the planners of Vatican I was to consider the Church as a whole: pope, bishops, other clergy, and all members. But the outcome was an unbalanced treatment of only the pope's power and place, an outcome which seemed to many to endorse a heavily monarchical and triumphant papacy.

Following Vatican I and prior to Vatican II, certain papal decrees and other developments offered only minor treatment of the nature of the Church as a whole.

When Vatican II was called, therefore, most observant theologians and bishops assumed rightly that this matter would be foremost on the agenda. During the council itself, when it seemed that the Roman Curia might succeed in derailing the discussion, Pope Paul VI himself reasserted his intention to have this council proceed where Vatican I had not.

The council fathers approved *Lumen Gentium* by a final vote of 2,151 to 5! The pope promulgated the document on November 21, 1964, during the third year of the council. *Lumen Gentium* holds a central place among council documents and has been received by the Church with nearly universal acclaim. It has been argued that, in fact, all the remaining council documents flow from this one, that all the others deal with an aspect of the Church (such as Liturgy, the missions, laypeople, or ecumenism) while this one sets forth the fundamental understanding of the Church itself. For example, chapter three of *Lumen Gentium* treats the hierarchy, setting forth fundamental principles of theology. Later council documents developed this theme, including separate documents on bishops, the life and ministry of priests, and seminary training.

Chapter four of *Lumen Gentium* deals with the place and role of the laity in the Church, a theme later expanded in a separate document on the laity.

Portions of *Lumen Gentium* also deal with missionary activity, ecumenism, religious life, and Liturgy, all themes taken up and developed more thoroughly by other council documents. None of the rest of the council's work would have been possible, therefore, had not the debate on this document occurred when it did.

Although the council's work is complete and Vatican II is officially ended and closed, the discussion on this matter is not ended. In fact, many issues raised in the council were only exploratory for the bishops involved. Many topics were mentioned only briefly and remain to be more fully developed. The Church's understanding of the meaning and theology of *Lumen Gentium* will continue to unfold in the life of the Church little by little.

Its centrality among council outcomes, its long history of development beginning with Vatican I, and its near unanimous acceptance by members of the Church might surprise anyone who knows how this document read when it was first presented to the council fathers for debate in 1962 during the first session.

Possibly no other council document underwent as much revision from the first draft to the last as this one. Thus, a brief telling of the story of the council's debate on this document is in order. (These notes are drawn from three principal sources: the daybooks of the council itself; the reports of Xavier Rynne in his book *Vatican Council II*, published by Farrar, Straus and Giroux in 1968; and articles in *Vatican II: An Interfaith Appraisal,* edited by John Miller and published by University of Notre Dame Press in 1966.)

The first draft was presented to the council on December 1, 1962, by Cardinal Alfredo Ottaviani, whose theological commission had prepared it. The draft consisted of a booklet containing two documents, both proposed as constitutions, one on the nature of the Church and another on the Blessed Virgin Mary.

Ottaviani praised the merits of the schema but also noted bitterly that he foresaw disagreements about his work. Aware that many of the world's bishops thought that authority in the Church should be shared among the bishops and the pope (decreasing thereby the authority held by the Roman Curia), the cardinal expected a difficult debate.

He could not have been more correct.

Indeed, as his commission's draft was being presented, an alternative draft, which many wanted as the basis of discussion on the matter, was already circulating on the council floor. Moreover, the discussion on the official schema as presented by Ottaviani was not positive. In fact, in its first form, the council fathers did not approve of it as even a basis for discussion. They wanted a much more progressive development of the understanding of the Church.

The major objections to the first draft were voiced loudly and clearly. Some council fathers objected to the first draft's emphasis on the hierarchy. Others wanted a chapter developing the notion of the Church as the People of God, which was omitted from the first draft. Still others suggested that the document on Mary be incorporated into a single, unified document on the Church. Some noted that there was no treatment of the end times or the relationship of the living to those who have died. There was also a discussion of the need to incorporate a chapter on religious life amid those on clergy and laity.

Many felt that the document as first presented did not provide enough of a theological basis for an understanding of the Church as a mystery and too much of an understanding of the Church as a society on earth.

Council fathers also rejected the long-held Catholic point of view regarding membership in the Church. With pressure from many theologians, including Karl Rahner, as well as from ecumenical circles and from the desires of Pope John XXIII himself, a more open definition was sought, one that would include people of goodwill, whether or not they were in full communion with Rome.

Perhaps the strongest criticism came from those who felt that the first draft ignored the relationship of bishops, deacons, priests, and laypeople. Vatican I had left questions about this open. The council fathers wanted a fuller treatment of how authority is shared in the Church and how collegiality plays a role in that. They were not in the mood to wait another hundred years for this to be included!

In response to this draft, a major movement was under foot. This movement would separate the questions on the nature of the Church itself from those on the relationship of the Church to the modern world. Eventually that was done and there are, as a result, two constitutions on the Church from Vatican II.

In general, the first draft presented by Cardinal Ottaviani was seen as a defense of the status quo in the Church when most council fathers seemed ready to advance the Church's understanding of itself.

At the end of the first session on December 7, 1962, the first draft was sent back to its commission for revision, under new directives from Pope John. These directives allowed members of the preparatory commissions to invite theological experts who were not bishops to join them in their work.

Meeting between sessions, the commission members agreed that the first draft was unsuitable as a basis for its revision and four other drafts were prepared as possible substitutes. One from Monsignor Parente was considered incomplete; one from the German theologians was considered too heavy; one from Cardinal Silva and other Brazilians was considered too much like the original. In the end, it was one from the French and Belgian theologians on which the commission chose to work.

Why? Because the new Franco-Belgian version was more in keeping with the suggestions of the council fathers which emerged in the first session. There was, for example, an exposition of the Church as the People of God preceding any commentary on specific roles among these people (lay, clergy, or religious). A new emphasis on the universal call to holiness also appeared. No decisions were taken at this point about where to place the statements on Mary or on the Church in heaven.

During the debates that followed this revision, speakers focused on (1) the People of God and the roles of the faithful as priestly, prophetic, and royal; (2) the question of the role of bishops in relationship to the pope; and (3) the reestablishment of a permanent diaconate without the obligation of celibacy. It also became clear during this period that they would add a chapter on Mary to the document rather than let the topic stand alone.

During this period, there were more than five hundred speeches resulting in more than 2,000 pages of testimony (not counting the debates on two later chapters which occurred in the third session of the council).

Eventually, voting began on the outcomes of all this debate and revision, and even though a small minority firmly opposed the statements on shared authority, the document as a whole, including that section, was approved with near unanimity.

As you read this document in its paraphrased format, remember that several different views of the Church run through the text. There were varying views of the Church at the council itself, of course. A simple linear reading of the text will be helpful to those of you who wish to understand its length and breadth. But it might also help you to put the book down in your lap from moment to moment and pause to ask about a section, "What does that *mean* to me today?"

If you want to do more reading on the background and meaning of the *Dogmatic Constitution on the Church*, consult the brief reading list in Appendix Two. Moreover, the paraphrase presented in this chapter provides the article numbers throughout to allow you to return to an original translation for a look at the actual texts of the primary source.

When returning to the original translations, try not to read a particular article in isolation from those around it or even from the entire chapter in which it is located. Precisely because varying views of the Church are represented, there is a danger in reading too little of the document and thereby encountering only one or another of those perspectives.

Finally, there is enough material in this document alone to set a discussion agenda for several years in parishes or other groups where members of the Church or friends want to learn more about the Church. Pastoral councils, parish leadership groups, ministry committees, social and volunteer groups—all can have access to the powerful texts produced under the guidance of the Holy Spirit at Vatican II.

Let us allow this same Spirit to penetrate us now with its wisdom, its desire for us to know God more fully, and its constant renewal of the Church!

PART TWO: PARAPHRASE TEXT

*F*rom the Second Vatican Council
proclaimed by Pope Paul VI on November 21, 1964

Introduction

1 Christ is the Light of the Nations:
    Lumen Gentium!
Because this is so,
        we bishops of the world,
        gathered by the Holy Spirit
        at this Second Vatican Council,
        eagerly desire to bring this Light
            to people everywhere
            by making the Gospel accessible
                to all of creation.
The Church is in Christ;

it is a sacrament of Christ,
a mystery of depth.
It is both a sign and an instrument
of intimate union with God
and of the total union of humans to one another.
And, therefore, the Church now wants to share
with the whole world
its own inner nature and mission.
This document does that.
In doing so it remains faithful to previous councils
while at the same time
taking stock of these times.
Our world society is wonderfully united today
by technology and culture.
But that alone is not enough
to fulfill our human destiny.
And, in fact, such secular unity
only makes it all the more urgent
that we should also come to full human unity
in Christ.
Lumen Gentium!

Chapter One
THE MYSTERY OF THE CHURCH

2 With a most profound wisdom and goodness,
God created the whole world
and from among all of creation
God chose us humans to share in the divine life,
to have an eternal walk with God
arm in arm
heart to heart.

And although we have stumbled along
    and at times have even lost our way,
    God has not abandoned us.
Instead, God remained radically present,
    eventually expressing the depth of parental love
        through Jesus Christ.

3 Jesus Christ is the one around whom the Church gathers.

Since the very beginning of time,
    God has been preparing this Church
    to receive Christ,
    both in the ancient covenant
        with the people of Israel
        as well as in this age of the Holy Spirit.
At the end of time, all of God's plans
    will finally be brought to completion.
Then the Church will be a gathering
    of all who believe in Christ
    and all who have ever sought goodness.
        Salvation!

By being joined to Christ,
    all of us were made children of God,
    sons and daughters of the one who created us,
        united in Jesus Christ.
Thus, the Reign of God on earth was inaugurated.

By Christ's obedience and love,
    our relationship with God was restored.
Thus, too, Christ's realm here on earth,
    which is fully present but seldom recognized,
    grows brighter and more visible
        as God's power unfolds.

Celebrating Eucharist over and over
    allows this power to unfold in the world
    and brings about our salvation.
Celebrating Eucharist over and over
    forms the Body of Christ,
    a unity into which everyone on earth is welcomed,
        a unity in Christ
        who is the Light of the World.
           Lumen Gentium!

4 And now in our own age,
    we have the Holy Spirit to guide us.
This Spirit is a fountain of living water
    springing up to life eternal!
The Spirit guides the Church in truth
    and continually makes the Church more holy.
Working through the ordinary lives of us all,
    the Spirit gives the Church everything it needs
    both for leadership and service
        and thus allows the Church
        to keep its youthful energy.
Praying through the hearts of the faithful
    and dwelling in us as in a temple,
    the Spirit unifies us all in love.
And therefore,
    we can say that we, the Church,
    are a people united by our common heritage:
        created in love by God,
        assembled in the name of Jesus,
        and bound together in the Holy Spirit.
The same power that mysteriously unites
    this threefold divine presence
    also binds us together in love.

5 We are at a loss to explain this wonderful divine mystery
    and to understand it fully
    no matter how long and faithfully we plumb it.
That's because it is a mystery of depth,
    not misunderstanding.
The Church itself is a mystery like this
    which can be understood, therefore,
    only by coming to know its very foundation:
        Jesus Christ.
Begun by his preaching the Good News
    which had been promised for centuries,
    this Church was enlivened and illuminated
        by the words,
            the works,
            the miracles,
            the very person of Jesus Christ.
To better understand the Church,
    we use symbols and metaphors
    that come from sacred Scripture.
The Word of God is like a seed, for example,
    planted by a farmer.
Those who hear the Word which became flesh in Christ
    actually live in the Reign of God here and now,
    a seed sprouting in them and growing to its harvest.
Christ's mission is that we might all have that seed
    planted within us
    and develop the inner spiritual energy to let it grow.
The Church now takes up the work of Christ,
    guided by the Holy Spirit,
    and continues to sow that seed of faith.

6 Using other metaphors and images,
    both the Hebrew Scriptures

and our own Testament of Gospels and letters
    also describe the Church
    to help us understand this.
In one place, it is compared
    to a flock of sheep with its shepherd;
    in another, to a field being cultivated by the farmer;
    and in yet another, to a relationship between lovers
        budding into romance and passion.
Sometimes it is referred to as a vineyard
    where the vine delivers life-giving sap
        to each branch
        to nourish it and make it fruitful.

Other times, the Church is called a building
    with Christ as the cornerstone.
    Here is where the household of God is found,
        the family united by its parents.
    Here is the temple where God dwells,
        the heartbeat of a heavenly city
        where each of us is a living stone
        together forming this dwelling place of God.
And perhaps the most touching metaphor in Scripture
    is the one where Christ is called our very spouse,
        ready to give us radical love,
        a love that surpasses everything we know.
7 But for us Catholics and for all people,
    the most central and clear message we have
    emerges from the metaphor
        where we come to understand
        that we are family.
We are indeed brothers and sisters,
    because of the life and death
    that Christ offered on our behalf.
We are, in fact, the very Body of Christ!

But what does this mean,
    to call ourselves the "Body of Christ"?

First, it means that we are united to Christ
    in a remarkable way because of baptism,
    which forms us in Christ's image.
In baptism, every aspect of Christ's being:
    life, death, resurrection
        takes root in us,
            body and soul.
And, second, in the Eucharist,
    that which was begun in baptism
    is constantly nourished and affirmed.
In the Eucharist, we experience real communion,
    true fellowship,
    and undeniable connectedness
        with Christ and with all people.
By these two sacraments we become
    full members of the Church,
    and members of the Body of Christ.
What we're actually saying here
    is that the Church is this Body.
Life in this Church is sometimes messy
    because the Church includes everyone
    with all their various talents and desires.
We would end up in a mess with all this
    if we did not have Christ to lead us.

How does this work?
    How does Christ lead the Church?
    The answer is both simple and complex,
        and a large part of this document
        deals with it.
Christ wants us to love each other,

to endure sorrow with one another,
to share happiness,
to forgive each other freely,
all in a family-like lifestyle.
Therefore, whoever leads us as the Church
toward a community filled with love,
greater and greater love,
real love lived out in everyday life,
that person speaks for Christ.
That person is leading the Church in the name of Christ.
There are many such leaders,
each with his or her own diverse function.
Many people have gifts for leadership
and offer them to the Church.
As Catholics, we believe that all this love,
all these talents and desires
are given "holy order" and made effective
through the unity we have
under the authority of the pope and bishops.
The presence of all these gifts,
unified and directed by the Church,
forms the way in which Christ and the Holy Spirit
lead the Church
and give it everything it needs
to serve the world today.
Thus, Christ leads the Church as its head,
and the Holy Spirit sustains the Church
as its soul.
We, then, as members of this Body
must be conformed to the image of Christ
and the Holy Spirit of God.
We must be directed by our head, Jesus Christ,
and by our soul, the Holy Spirit.
In this way,

we serve one another unto salvation,
which means that by loving each other
we give each other the opportunity
to be embraced by God
and live with God eternally.

8 Given all this,
we can clearly see now that Christ both
established and sustains the Church on earth
which is a community of faith,
hope,
and love.
We do not distinguish between the Body of Christ
which we have just described
and the organized Church
with its structures and leaders.
This is complex but can be understood this way:
there is in the Church
both a human and a divine element.
It is like Christ's own nature,
which is both human and divine.
This divine and human nature of the Church,
where mystery and plainness swim together,
where the social structures swim
with the Spirit of God,
is the one Church of Christ.
It is indeed one,
and it is also holy, universal, and apostolic.
Part of the social structure given this Church by Christ
is the leadership of Peter,
who was commissioned as a shepherd,
along with the other apostles,
whose jobs were to help maintain
this delicate truth

that the Church is indeed the Body of Christ.
And while this Church,
    organized in the world as a society,
    is found in the Catholic Church,
        many elements of truth and holiness
        are also found outside its structures.
These elements outside the Catholic Church
    are part of what urges us
    to desire greater unity among Christians.

We who claim to be the Church,
    we who claim to be the Body of Christ,
    must resemble Christ as much as possible.
We must take the part of the poor whenever we can;
    we must defend those without power;
    we must avoid seeking our own glory
        and act with humility and self-sacrifice
        for the good of all.
We who are Christian
    and, indeed, the organized Church itself
    must take in those who are afflicted,
        forgotten,
        and suffering.
The Church itself, like its members,
    is always in need of being renewed and forgiven,
        purified for its mission,
        which is the same as the mission of Christ.
And if we are faithful in this way,
    as an organized Church
    and as its individual members,
    we will succeed in announcing Christ to the world
        until all is seen in full light.
            Lumen Gentium!

Chapter Two
ON THE PEOPLE OF GOD

9 God has always welcomed anyone
  whose heart is ready to experience
  the divine presence.
These are the ones whose lives reflect goodness
  and who cultivate a sense of awe.
But God has also always chosen
  to welcome women and men,
  not merely as individuals
    but bound together,
    united as a people who recognize the divine.
So, coming together as a people
  is an essential element of salvation.
Hence, the house of Israel came as one people,
  united in a covenant with God,
  slowly growing more and more ready
    to receive God fully,
    ready to live within a full and new covenant.
In Christ, this new covenant was instituted,
  and all were called together as a people:
  both Jew and Gentile,
    united in one common Spirit.
This would be "a chosen race,"
  as the First Letter of Peter calls it,
  "a royal priesthood,
    a holy nation,
    the people of God."
This people, which we call the Church,
  has Christ as its head,
  as we have said already.
This people has the dignity and freedom
  of the sons and daughters of God.

Its law is the commandment to love
as Christ, the great Lover, loves us.
Its end is the Reign of God
begun now here on earth
and set to last for eternity.
Not all people belong to this Church,
yet all people are included in the reach
of its embrace.
The challenges and tasks that face the Church
appear overwhelming at times.
Nonetheless, we are like a seed
that will surely someday
bear the fruit of unity,
hope,
and healing for all.
The Church is constantly moving and searching,
wandering . . .
not unlike the Hebrew experience in the desert.
And even though the Church's movement
is sometimes filled with trial and tribulation,
nonetheless, it remains faithful overall.
It continues to be a visible sign of unity,
a sacrament of salvation for all people.
Aware of the absolute importance of its mission,
the Church seeks constant renewal.
It never ceases to beg the Holy Spirit
for the grace it needs
to be the Light of the World.
Lumen Gentium!

10 The baptized members of the Church,
because they are consecrated by the Holy Spirit,
share in the priesthood of Jesus Christ.
In the widest sense, a priest is anyone

who makes the world and its people holy
by sacrificing and praying on its behalf.
In this sense,
every single baptized person is a priest.
As priests, therefore, all the faithful are called
to offer themselves to God
and to offer the hope of God
to one another.
They should, therefore, be faithful in prayer
and live as part of the household of God.

We make a distinction, however,
between the priesthood of the baptized
and the priesthood of those ordained for ministry.

The ordained priest is charged to
shape and bring holy order
to the whole priestly people of God.
The ministry of the ordained is to teach and serve all people.
Precisely because ordained priests are the ones
whose job is to give the Church order,
they act in the person and the power of Christ
when they preside at Eucharist.
Those in the baptized priesthood also join
in offering the Eucharist.
They, too, serve in a priestly way
by participating in the sacraments,
by praying and offering thanks to God,
and by graciously serving their sisters and brothers.

11 In fact, the ideals of this priestly community
become a reality when the members
celebrate the sacraments
and exercise habits of goodness.

Baptism and confirmation identify Christians
    as daughters and sons of God,
    willing to give their lives to the Church
    that others might experience the friendship of Christ.
Eucharist provides them with
    the deepest source of strength
    and the highest moment of spiritual insight.
Reconciliation helps them focus on the mercy of God.
The sacred anointing of the sick
    lightens the load of suffering which they bear.
Those called to holy orders
    are appointed to feed the Church in Christ's name
    with the Word and the grace of God.
And those called to matrimony
    live especially close to the unity and fruitful love
    that exists between Christ and the Church.
In fact, those who receive this sacrament,
    by reason of their state and rank in life,
    have their own special gift
        among the People of God.
From their lovemaking comes forth
    new citizens of the world,
    those who will also ultimately live in the light.
This family setting is its own kind of Church,
    a sort of "domestic" Church.
In this household setting,
    where relationships are the stuff of daily life,
    for better or for worse,
        members ought to witness to each other
        and teach each other to listen to the Spirit
            prompting them in their hearts.

12 When this whole Church,
    anointed as it is by the Holy Spirit,

believes together,
  the truth of the faith is absolutely undeniable.
It is like a chalice overflowing with so much truth
  that even when everyone drinks from it,
    it becomes fuller
    rather than emptier.
Such belief is ratified and declared through the leaders,
  making everyone able to believe together.
This faith becomes clearer,
  more meaningful,
  more believable to others
    when believers practice it
    in every aspect of their daily lives.
This same Spirit likewise sanctifies the whole world,
  which means that through the Spirit
  every aspect of the world will eventually be brought
    to goodness and holiness.
This will happen because the Spirit gives gifts
  to each person and assists each
    in using them well.
The power we need to do this
  comes only from God
  and leads us insistently to more and more
    become exactly who we are created to be.
We call this shared, loving, sacred power
  by a name: we call it "grace."
Grace is, then, "the energy of God in our lives,"
  the loving presence of the divine one.
It is given to everyone at every rank of the Church.
It forms us into a community
  which also has a name: the People of God!

13 All people everywhere and throughout all time
  are called to belong to this People of God.

And doesn't this fit God's way of doing things?
God did, after all, create us in the divine image
    to share human nature together.
Together we share an inescapable sameness.
God even became one of us in Jesus Christ
        so that we might be united as human beings,
            that we might begin to realize
            that this sameness is a wonderful gift.

But human unity may seem like a far-off dream.
    Our experience of national tensions
    and cultural warfare
        makes such worldwide unity
        appear impossible!

God's Reign, however, is not like an earthly one
        because it encompasses citizens of every race
            with all their various cultures
            and it forms these people into a Church.
In accepting these gifts of every nation,
        both spiritual and temporal,
        and uniting them into the one Family of God,
        the Church does not diminish the welfare of anyone.
On the contrary, it seeks to increase good everywhere.
Hence we call the Church "catholic,"
        a Greek word that means "universal."
        This means that all parts contribute to all others
            and share their gifts in common.

14 Everyone on earth is welcomed into this unity,
        and each is called in a unique way.
For those called to be Catholic,
        the Church is necessary for salvation,
        according to both Scripture and tradition.

We believe that for the Catholic faithful
    the Church is necessary for salvation
    because it is in the Church that we encounter Christ,
        who is "the Way."
Any Catholic who knows this
    and freely chooses to reject or leave the Church
        may ultimately also be choosing
        to reject salvation.
Not only that,
    being fully part of the Church means that we
    embrace all the Church has to offer:
        creed,
        sacraments,
        community,
        and authority.
Beyond that, we must also live in love.
The failure to put love into practice,
    even if we are faithful to the Church
    in all other ways, is a rejection of salvation itself.
This is a sin that is serious enough
    to bring about severe judgment.
Those called to be catechumens are embraced as family
    as soon as the Holy Spirit stirs up in them
    the desire and will for full participation
        in the life of the Church.

[15] Those called to be Christians in other churches
    and with whom the pope is not yet fully united
    are nonetheless linked to the Church in many ways.
United to Roman Catholics by Scripture,
        prayer,
        charity,
        and even sacraments,
    together we hope and work toward full unity.

The Church urges all its members to lives
    that are holy and renewed to enable this.

16 And the many people who are not Christian
    are also connected to the People of God.
The Jews remain dear to God, for example,
    as do the people of Islam,
        as well as all those who seek God
        with a sincere heart.
Likewise, those who seek no God whatsoever,
    if they are good and true,
    are also related to God's People.
        Only those who persist in darkness
        and cultivate despair
            have cut off their relationship
            to the People of God.

17 Following the desire and command of Christ,
    the Church makes a serious effort
    to present the Gospel to the whole world
        so that people can share in God's love.
Everyone who is baptized is charged with this mission.
The Church works and prays diligently
    with great hope
    that everyone in the whole world
        will ultimately join together
        as the People of God.

Chapter Three
ON THE HIERARCHICAL STRUCTURE OF THE CHURCH, IN PARTICULAR THE BISHOPS

18 As we have said,
　　Christ instituted a variety of ministries
　　　　within the Church
　　　　for the good of the whole Body.
Among these is the role of bishop,
　　which flows from the relationship of Jesus
　　to his closest apostles,
　　　　with Peter as their leader.
We believe that Christ wants these leaders
　　and their successors
　　to continue in their roles for all time.
And we also want to lay out plainly here
　　what the role of the bishop is
　　and how bishops work with each other
　　　　and with the pope
　　　　to guide and direct
　　　　　　the household of God.

19 Jesus prayerfully called an initial twelve apostles
　　whose sole desire was to spend their lives
　　　　in his presence.
Thus Jesus formed a permanent community of leadership,
　　a sort of "college" with them.
They were eventually sent out to teach,
　　　　preach,
　　　　heal,
　　　　and minister to the people of that age.
They were sent to spread the faith
　　to all the world.
And they were confirmed in this mission

by the Holy Spirit at Pentecost,
as Acts of the Apostles tells us.

Eventually they came to be called "bishops."

20 These first ones appointed by Christ
soon added others, and down through history
such appointments have continued
so that since the time of Jesus
there has been a steady succession of bishops,
passing on the mantle of ministry and leadership
and continuing the work of Christ.
With priests and deacons to help them,
the bishops preside over the People of God,
taking the place of the apostles
in doing so.
Whoever listens to them
is listening to Christ.

21 The authority that bishops exercise requires
wisdom,
understanding,
and sincerity of heart.
These gifts are given to a bishop in his ordination
and become operative
as he puts them into practice.

The primary role of the bishop
is to be a shepherd for God's People,
helping them to maintain a sense
of order, harmony, and unity.
To do this,
bishops receive a special outpouring
of the Holy Spirit

passed to them
through the laying on of hands
in their ordination.
This gives them what we call
"the fullness of the priesthood,"
meaning they are named as those
who take the place of Christ for us.

22 Bishops are not free agents;
they are bound together as a college,
speaking in unity with the pope,
in a bond of charity and peace.
Together with the pope,
who is the successor of Peter
and the bishop of Rome,
the bishops are called to reflect
perfect unity among themselves.
Maintaining this unity of faith and unity of heart
among Catholic people
is an extremely important aspect of the Church.
This Second Vatican Council reaffirms this
by clearly enunciating
the importance of the role of the bishops
and their relation to the pope.

As such, the gathering of this very council
expresses a model of operating for the Church.
In this model, the opinion of the many
is prudently considered
when making decisions about important matters.
We have a long history of holding councils
such as this one
where we consider major questions together.
An ecumenical council, however,

has no authority unless it speaks in one voice
    with the bishop of Rome.
It is infallible if and only if it teaches
    in unity with the pope.
Ultimately, the bishop of Rome
    has authority over all bishops,
    and is pastor of the universal Church.

23 Individual bishops likewise serve as a sign of unity
    in their own dioceses where they work.
They are also concerned
    with the welfare of the whole Church.

24 The ministry of the bishop is one of service
    to those among whom he stands.

25 In the local diocese,
    the bishop is the authentic teacher
    of faith and morals,
    and the faithful are to accept his teaching.
Toward this end, preaching the Gospel
    holds the first priority.
Bishops preach and teach this way,
    in union with the pope
    and under his watchful concern.

26 Bishops are responsible for seeing to it
    that the people in the dioceses they serve
    have the opportunity
        to celebrate the sacraments,
        especially the Eucharist.
The Church is fully present
    in all local groups of the faithful
    when the group is organized legitimately

and united to its pastor.
Christ is fully present in each of these "altar communities"
    because Christ is present
    whenever the Eucharist is celebrated.
Each local community, therefore,
    is a microcosm of the whole Church,
        fully reflecting the goodness of God
        and suffering the difficulties of everyday life.
Hence, among the official duties of bishops
    are the tasks of caring for the poor and lonely
    and assisting other dioceses in need of help.
Bishops pray and toil for the people,
    and through the sacraments,
    they give the faithful everything needed
        to attain salvation.

27 By their manner of life,
    their advice to the faithful,
    and their exhortations,
        bishops lead their people.
Theirs is a humbling power
    meant only to lead others
    to spiritual development.
They are not vicars of the pope
    but vicars of Christ himself!
Their model, therefore, is that of the Good Shepherd,
    who came to serve
    and not be served,
        who came to lay down his life
        for his flock!
For their part, the faithful should be kindly disposed
    toward their bishops!

28 It would be humanly impossible for any one bishop

to do everything needed in the Church.
Therefore, God has established
    three levels of ordained ministry:
        bishop,
        priest,
        and deacon.

Priests participate in the ministry of the bishop.
They are consecrated to preach the Gospel,
    shepherd the faithful in unity,
    and celebrate divine worship.
Their most visible and important role
    is that of presiding at the Eucharist.
In this ministry, they are most tightly connected to
    the person of Christ
        and the mission of their bishop.
They labor in Word and doctrine,
    believing what they have read and mediating on that,
    teaching what they believe,
    and putting into practice in their own lives
        what they have taught.
Working with their bishops,
    priests strive to lend their effort to the pastoral work
    of the whole diocese and even of the entire Church.
They share an intimate brotherhood with each other,
    offering one another mutual aid,
        spiritual and material,
        pastoral and personal.
Priests are to look after the spiritual needs
    of the parishes entrusted to them
    with the concern of a caring father
        who tends his family with love.
Through their daily conduct and care,
    they have a truly priestly and pastoral ministry

both to believers and nonbelievers,
  to Catholics and non-Catholics.

29 In the very early years of the Church,
    deacons, too, participated in the ministry
    of their bishop.
However, over the centuries
    the diaconate has fallen into disuse.
Because of the needs of the world,
    this council now gives approval
        to the restoration of the diaconate.
Deacons have a ministry of service
    to administer solemn baptism,
    dispense the Eucharist,
    witness marriages,
    bring *viaticum* to the dying,
    read the Scriptures to the faithful,
    administer sacramentals,
    officiate at funerals,
    and be dedicated to charity and administration.
Under the rules of the restored diaconate,
    even married men can be ordained deacon.
    But if an unmarried man is ordained,
        he must remain celibate forever.

Chapter Four
THE LAITY

30 It is clear that bringing order to the Church
    and keeping us all moving together
    on the right path
        requires a well-ordered system.

Toward this end, members of the hierarchy—
    bishops, priests, and deacons—
    have a clearly defined
        and quite specific role
        within the Church.
Less defined, but equally important, is the role
    of those called to be members of the laity.
This Second Vatican Council now eagerly outlines
    the indispensable role of the layperson.

31 When we speak of "the laity,"
    we include all the baptized members of the Church
    except sisters, brothers, and clergy.
32 There are some matters that pertain specifically
    to lay women and men,
    but everything said above about the People of God
        applies equally to everyone in the Church.
The pastors of the Church
    know how much the laity contributes to the welfare
        of the Church and of the world.
They also know that they should not try
    to do everything themselves
    because that is not their ordained role.
Among laypeople, sisters, brothers, and the ordained
    there exists a harmony and balance:
        cooperation and collaboration.
Such working together is essential
    if the Church is to become
    the "salt of the earth."

34 As the role of the ordained priest
    is to consecrate bread and wine
    to be the Body and Blood of Christ,
        so the role of the layperson

is to consecrate the entire world!

36 While the ordained concern themselves
    with bringing "holy order" to the Church,
    the layperson is concerned with
    bringing "holy order" to the world.
Thus, the laity are entrusted with the important job
    of ordering the world's goods
    so that all people are cared for
        and no one is overlooked.
There is in Christ
    complete equality regardless of race,
        nationality,
        social condition,
        and gender.

It is up to the laypeople to oversee
    the customs and conditions of the world.
    Let them order these according to the norms
        of justice,
        peace,
        and the dignity of all.

33 Thus, the vocation of each layperson
    is to seek the Reign of God
    in his or her everyday work
        and to direct that work
        according to God.
34 Laypeople live in ordinary circumstances
    of family and social life,
    which is where they are called by God.
By their lifestyles
    their work,
    their prayer,

their family life,
their leisure and entertainment,
and their hardships too
    laypeople give witness
    to the Light of Christ.
35 The laity go forth as powerful proclaimers
    of a faith in things to be hoped for.
36 All Christians, especially those
    who share the special sacrament of married life,
    loudly proclaim this faith:
        the presence of the Reign of God,
        the hope of blessings to come.
In doing so, they must wrestle and stand against
    all in this world
        that is not of God.
It is the responsibility of laypeople
    to maintain the delicate and subtle balance
    between Church and society.

33 They must not force every aspect of the Church
    upon the rest of the world
    nor can they neglect the wisdom and goodness
        that the Church can offer to society.
Every lay person is, therefore,
    at the same time a witness
    and a living instrument of the mission
        of the Church itself.
The laity receive from Christ and from the Church
    everything that is necessary to fulfill their vocation.
35 From Christ, they receive an authentic sense of faith,
    an inner voice
        which sounds the call of truth,
        and the Word of God
            which directs this truth.

37 Thus laypeople have the obligation
    to constantly develop a more profound grasp
        of their Christian faith.
Laypeople also receive
    spiritual goods from the Church
        and from their pastors.
38 Since they need these spiritual goods to fulfill their call,
    such goods are not only a privilege
    but a right as well.
In order to receive what they really need,
    they must express their needs and wants openly.
They must be attentive to the direction of the Church
    and play a part in providing leadership.
There are even times
    when laypeople have a serious obligation
    to express their opinions and insights
        about the Church.
Their wisdom and knowledge
    often arise from valuable life experience.
Such wisdom is to be prized by church leaders.
When laypeople challenge the Church,
    it should be through official channels
        and with courage,
        respect,
        and above all, charity.
In the end, laypeople should embrace
    as fully as possible
    what their pastors decide.

It is extremely important that laypeople
    pray for their pastors.

Pastors must likewise pray for their parishioners,
    trust their wisdom,

and take to heart all they have to say.
They should be open
    to all the different talents, gifts, and experiences
      that laypeople bring to the Church.
Pastors must give real responsibility to parishioners
    and encourage them
      to take initiative in their parishes.
Such authentic trust and cooperation
    between the laity and their spiritual leaders
    holds great potential for the Church:
Laypeople will take greater ownership in the Church
    and gain renewed enthusiasm
    for wholehearted cooperation
      with their pastors.
The ordained will likewise be better equipped
    to make wise decisions
    regarding both spiritual and temporal matters.

In the end,
    the Christian layperson must be to the world
    what the soul is to the body.

Chapter Five
THE UNIVERSAL CALL TO HOLINESS
IN THE CHURCH

[39] The Church is holy.
    The Church was holy.
      The Church will always be holy.
We know this to be true because
    Christ loved the Church into holiness
    and gave her the presence of the Holy Spirit.

This holiness is made evident
    by the many women and men
    who draw from the Church
        the spirit and strength
        to live lives of holy goodness.
40 We are called to holiness by Christ himself,
    who taught, in the words of St. Matthew,
    that we must be "perfect as God is perfect."
By transforming the activities and events
    of everyday life into holy moments,
    all the faithful grow in this perfection
    and the world more and more resembles God's Reign.

So it is clear that everyone,
    lay,
    religious,
    and ordained,
is called to be holy.

"Love God with all your heart,"
    the Scriptures tell us,
        "with all your soul,
        with all your understanding,
        with all your strength.
Love one another as Christ loves you."
These commands in Scripture
    are really an invitation to be holy.
By our holy love, we nurture in the world
    a way of life that is more gentle,
        more beautiful,
          more human.
Over and over again,
    the Scriptures describe for us
    what this holiness will resemble:

a heart of mercy,
humility,
meekness,
patience,
awareness of God's mercy
when we have sinned,
and a spirit of forgiveness toward others.

41 There are many ways to live out this call to be holy.
Everyone should walk
according to his or her own personal gifts
and duties,
in the pathway of a living faith.
Bishops are to be so faithful to this call
that they would lay down their lives
for the people that they serve.
Priests have the special duty
to make prayer
an integral part of their daily lives,
thus making their service more authentic
and their sacrifice more genuine.
Deacons and other people called to church ministry
should model their lives after the apostles,
who worked tirelessly for the Gospel.
Married couples and parents
should sustain one another in grace
throughout the entire length of their lives.
Widows and single people likewise
give witness to their holiness through their labors
in the Church in society.
For those called to them,
the promises of chastity, obedience, and poverty
are also a means to holiness.
Others, particularly those who suffer,

the poor and the ill,
find holiness in their special relationship
with Christ who suffered.

42 Love is the principal way to holiness.
Beyond that and included within it are
the sacraments,
prayer,
the Eucharist,
self-sacrifice,
service to others,
and virtue lived every day.
Therefore, all the faithful of Christ
are invited to strive for holiness,
even perfection.
Let all hear God's call within them,
each one observant and appreciative
of life's unique treasures.
Let neither the use of the things of this world
nor attachment to riches
hinder them in their quest for perfect love.

Chapter Six
RELIGIOUS

43 Another way in which many women and men
choose to live out their baptismal call
is to be part of a religious order.
In doing so, they embrace the "evangelical counsels."
That is, they take vows
of poverty,
chastity,

and obedience.
Indeed, this is a "Gospel way of life,"
    for it is founded on the teaching
    and example of Christ.

Throughout its history,
        the Church has affirmed the evangelical counsels
        and recognized them as a profound gift.
The Church desires to promote this way of life
        and keep it safe from whatever would harm it,
        either from the outside or from within.
Therefore, the Church is concerned
        about those called to this way of life.
It assists them in forming lasting commitments
        to their communities
        and in keeping the ideals of poverty,
                chastity,
                and obedience
                        in their proper perspective.
There are many forms of religious life.

Some live in community,
        while others live in solitude.
There are religious orders
        of sisters,
        brothers,
        laypeople,
        and priests.
All of them seek to embody
        the ideals of their founders
                and the Spirit of Jesus Christ.
The religious state of life
        is not an intermediate state
                between ordination and lay life.

Rather, it holds a place of its own in the Church
    and includes members of both clergy and laity.

44 A person enters the religious life
    by way of vows or promises,
        eventually committing herself or himself for life.
Indeed, in baptism everyone is called
    to live a life of holiness.
    These vows help an individual
        to put this baptismal call into practice.
Those who make such vows in religious life
    consecrate their entire lives to God
    in a very specific and public way.
In this form of radical Christian life,
    they have the freedom to serve God and the Church
    wherever they are needed most.

45 Religious orders are approved and promoted
    by the local bishop,
    thus assuring that there will be true cooperation
    between the various ministries
        that exist in a diocese.
46 They have a duty to work diligently
    to implant and strengthen the Reign of God
        in our times.
This can happen both through prayer
    and active apostolic labor.

Those living consecrated lives
    should remember well
    that both believer and nonbeliever
        find Christ in them daily.
In a concrete way, they demonstrate to the world
    how Jesus prayed privately on the mountain,

proclaimed the Reign of God to the crowds,
    healed the sick,
    worked to lead all to a better life,
    and lived in obedience
        to the One who sent him.
So let all the faithful realize
    that by committing themselves to these vows,
    women and men religious do not alienate themselves
    from other people or from the world.
Nor do they become useless members of our human society.
For even they who do not live and mingle
    among their contemporaries
    still maintain a strong spiritual bond
        with all other Christians.
This council encourages and praises
    those who generously offer themselves in service
        as religious sisters and brothers.

Chapter Seven
THE PILGRIM CHURCH
AND THE COMMUNION OF SAINTS

47 We are called to be together in the Church
    and, through God's grace in the Church,
        to achieve holiness.
But this Church is not yet perfectly holy
    and will not reach perfection until the end of time.
Then all creation will be restored in Christ.
Christ sent his life-giving Spirit to us
    after the Resurrection.
And even though Christ is now ascended to heaven,
    he remains actively among us in the Church

and present to us in his very Body and Blood.

Christ has already begun this restoration
 of our close ties to God
 and invited us to be part of it.
In the Church as we celebrate the sacraments,
 live in community,
 and serve one another,
  we learn the true meaning of our lives.
Through faith, we come to understand
 our unique role in bringing about this restoration
 by helping the world reflect God's goodness.

There is cause for great excitement here.
This new world has already begun,
 indeed is already here,
 and we are invited to be part of it.
There is also a tension here which we can clearly recognize:
 We know we are children of heaven
  because we have experienced it
  in beauty, relationships, and community.
Yet we still live with all the pain and difficulty
 of being children of the earth.
We are, indeed, sons and daughters of God
 while at the same time
 we are children of the earth
  waiting for even fuller unity with God.
God's love for us is so great and mysterious
 that we can glimpse only a little of it now.

48 Even the little we now see, however,
 is really awesome!
We believe that God's love is always waiting
 for us to receive it,

like water hidden by a dam,
a reservoir of love is poised
to flow out upon those who love.
And one day, at the time of death,
we hope to see and feel this divine love
in all its force and power.
So we should live in readiness and expectation
as though that might occur today,
because none of us knows for sure
when we will die.

The Scriptures are filled with images
of this Reign of God
and the day of God's return.
There is a kind of "final judgment day"
on which how we have chosen to live now
will stretch itself into eternity
as the pattern in which we will live forever.
To those who are strangers to God's love,
who have held an umbrella of spite all their lives,
such a flood of God's love will be frightening.
They will spend eternity in fear,
trying to escape from it.
Those who recognize God,
who have stood out in the Reign of God
loving and serving one another,
will gladly welcome God's abundant presence.
They will live in eternal goodness.

[49] At the present time, while all await God's full return,
some of the faithful live on earth,
some have died and are being purified,
and others live in glory with God.
But all of us are in one great communion,

bound together in God's love
    which is unbroken by death.
Those in heaven live fully with God,
    yet they remain united to us in love.
        They now serve God closely
        and know God completely.
Thus they add a dimension of holiness to the Church:
    They pray for us.
    They worship with us.
    They lend us their spiritual strength
        in our weakness.

50 Therefore, it is right and fitting
    for us to cultivate the memory of the dead:
        Mary,
        the apostles and martyrs,
        those whose poverty allowed them
            to understand God more completely,
        those whose virginity brought them
            into close companionship with God,
        and all the faithful who have died.
We remember those who have died
    because their lives inspire us
        to maintain hope
        in all that God has in store for us.
By following in their footsteps,
    we arrive at perfect union with Christ:
    we arrive, in a word,
        at "holiness."

Our ongoing union with our beloved dead
    is most powerful when we celebrate Liturgy.
In the Eucharist, the whole communion of Christ,
    living and dead,

gathers around the table.
At that moment, we are truly one great Church:
    the whole Body of Christ present
    in mystery and friendship.
It makes sense that in our experience of holy Eucharist,
    we experience a profound closeness
        with those who have gone before us.
For in the Eucharist, we receive
    the Body and Blood of Christ
    and thus we are fully united with Christ.
Those in heaven are most surely united with Christ too.

And here is a key point in all of this:
    We who live and pray on earth
    are not united with a "different" Christ
        than those who live and pray in heaven!
    No, there is one Christ,
        one Lord,
        who unites us all in love.
Truly the Eucharist is a marvelous gathering
    of heaven and earth!

51 This council affirms the ancient teachings of the Church
    regarding our relationship to those who have died
        and their important place in the Church.
But we also recognize that certain abuses have crept in
    and urge that they be corrected.
Our veneration of the saints,
    our fondness for those who have died,
    is not about miracles and other external acts.
It is about intensifying our practice of love.
Hence, a true and authentic remembering of the dead
    will enhance our worship
        and bring us closer to God.

In the end, judgment will be a glorious event.
    At that moment,
        the saints who have gone before us
        will be waiting to greet us.
    At that moment, we will be reunited
    with everyone we have ever loved,
        and with those whom we have hurt,
        we will stand reconciled.
Together we will not be able to stop singing to God,
    laughing,
        overwhelmed with peace.

    Joy will be so overpowering. . . .

Chapter Eight
THE BLESSED VIRGIN MARY
IN THE MYSTERY OF CHRIST AND THE CHURCH

52 God is ultimately wise and good
    and knows humankind intimately.
Before we speak,
    God knows the desires of our souls
    and how they are best fulfilled.
That is why God chose to send us Jesus Christ,
    Son of God and Savior.
Fully God and at the same time fully human.

Jesus did not come to us by magic.
Rather, God chose to make his coming into the world
    more reflective of God's inner self
        and God's relationship to humankind.
God wanted Jesus' presence to reflect

freedom,
commitment,
and divine intimacy.
And so, for the mother of Jesus,
God chose someone who was
free,
committed to faith,
and filled with God's love.

God chose Mary.
Mary chose God.

53 Because of this, we as Christians
can never take for granted
the gift that Mary presented to us
and nurtured for us:
the gift of divine love,
Jesus Christ.
For this we respect,
revere,
and honor Mary.
54 This council wants to make clear
what we as Catholics believe about Mary.
We want to describe her role in the Incarnation,
and we want to describe
how we can best respond to Mary.
In short, we want to nurture
a healthy relationship with Mary
by coming to understand
her proper role in the plan of salvation.

55 Mary is acknowledged as both
the Mother of God
and Mother of the Redeemer.

Because of this, she has a place of honor
    both in the Church and in heaven.

She has a unique relationship to God
    and a special relationship to the Church.
And although she is unlike us in these ways,
    she is also like us in the most fundamental aspects
        of her nature:
She is in need of salvation,
    not because of any sin,
    but simply because she is human.
Mary does not stand above Christ,
    but stands with all of us who need a savior.
What a remarkable relationship this is!
    Jesus depended on Mary
    for the things of this earth.
        Mary depended on Jesus
        for the things of heaven!

This, of course, means
    that Mary is a member of the Church
    and an excellent example of faith and charity.
We Catholics, therefore, honor her
    with childlike affection.

From the very beginning of time,
    God had something important planned for Mary.
The place of Mary in the plan of salvation
    is even foretold in the writings of Isaiah,
    a Hebrew prophet:
        "A virgin shall give birth to a son
        and the nations will call him Emmanuel,
            'God with us.'"
Yet though she was part of God's plan,

Mary was free to say yes or no to God.
Her role was not forced upon her.

56 Rather, God had great things in store for Mary,
and she freely chose to accept them.
That willingness on her part to serve
is an essential part of the working out of holiness,
the fight against sin in the world,
and the coming of the Holy Spirit.
It is no wonder that the earliest members of the Church
quickly developed a sense of awe
at Mary's place and role!
We believe God willed this:
that Mary's acceptance of the angel's call
would precede the conception of Jesus
and that Mary, a virgin forever,
would give birth to Emmanuel,
Jesus Christ.
This is often seen
as the reversal of the story of Adam and Eve:
By the actions of one man and one woman,
sin and suffering entered the world
and our relationship with God
was put in turmoil.
Jesus Christ, the new Adam,
restored grace to the world,
and Mary participated in this
through her loving cooperation
with God.

57 The New Testament has many examples of the unfolding
of this plan to save the world:
Elizabeth greeted Mary and called her "blessed,"
causing the infant to leap within her.

Jesus' birth left Mary fresh and fulfilled.
The spontaneous worship of the shepherds,
 the glorious visit of the magi,
 the presentation in the temple,
 the prophetic words of Simeon,
 and finally, Jesus being lost in the temple,
  and three days later found,
all of these were part of Mary's parental devotion and work,
 and all of them complete the unfolding story
  of the Incarnation.
58 Indeed, in Jesus' ministry,
 Mary was also present at key moments.
From Cana to the cross, Mary was present:
 faithful mother,
 faithful daughter of God.
59 After Jesus' death, Mary remained present:
 she persevered in prayer and waited in faith
  with the apostles and the other women
  who had also known Jesus.
And we believe Mary is now as close to Jesus as ever,
 present with God in heaven.

60 Christ is the one Mediator
 between God and humanity.
Because of the Holy Spirit,
 we have a direct friendship with Jesus,
 who can bring us into an intimate relationship
  with God.
Our devotion to Mary must never diminish that.
61 But since she played such a pivotal role
 in the life and work of Christ,
 we now realize that she is
 the first to receive the grace we also seek.
62 And even though Mary's place is subordinate to Christ's,

nonetheless, we still understand her
to be a great helper
on our way to holiness.
63 By her belief and obedience
and through the work of the Holy Spirit,
she gave birth to Jesus and raised him
with Joseph.
Her faith remained strong:
Even though she must have faced temptations
just like Adam and Eve,
and just like Jesus,
she listened instead to God's message.
64 Since Mary is the mother of Jesus
and we are sisters and brothers of Jesus,
we can call Mary our mother as well.
How appropriate this is,
and how privileged we are
to have such a mother,
one who is eternally attentive to our struggles
and always ready to nurture us spiritually!

The Church takes Mary as its example
and always tries to imitate her life
and always seeks to give birth
to the presence of Christ in the world.
Hence, the Church is also a mother to the faithful,
bearing Christ for them,
gently guiding them in life
to an entire faith,
a firm hope,
and sincere charity.

65 Therefore, the faithful now turn their eyes to Mary
as the model of virtue.

By meditating on her, we grow more and more like her son
    and enter more intimately into the mystery
        of the Incarnation.
We honor Mary
    and have a piety toward her
    so that we can better know Christ
        and the whole world can be more open
        to receiving the grace of Christ.

66 There is absolutely no other reason
    for our devotion to Mary.

67 At no time should our devotion to Mary
    resemble the reverence and worship
        that we give to God.
We encourage Catholics to foster a loving devotion
    for Mary
    as our custom has been for so many centuries.
But at the same time,
    this council urges theologians and pastors
    to abstain both from gross exaggerations
    and neglectful omission
        in considering the dignity of Mary.
Our piety should be based on both Scripture
    and the long-standing tradition of the Church
    and should follow Church teaching.
We should all be careful not to act in such a way
    that others will misunderstand us,
    especially other Christian Churches
        that might not foster
        such a strong devotion to Mary.

68–69 Mary's place is with God in heaven.
    This gives us great hope

of what we ourselves can look forward to.
And so with great longing
    and heartfelt trust,
    we bring our prayers to Mary
        and ask her to pray for us.
We know that she desires
    exactly what God desires
        and what we really want:
That in the end,
    all will be restored in Christ,
    and everyone will live in peace
        with God and with one another.
Then we will truly know what it means
    to be the People of God.
Then we will fully understand
    that Christ is the Light of the Nations.
        Lumen Gentium!

The Dogmatic Constitution on Divine Revelation

Dei Verbum

Chapter Two

PART ONE: BACKGROUND

*E*very action taken at the Second Vatican Council is based on the understanding of how God reveals Godself to people. Therefore, the contents of this brief and rather straight-forward document are essential to the work on all the others. For if Christians do not believe that what they teach is God's Word revealed to them and if they cannot convince others of this, how will the Gospel be preached in today's world?

The original schema was presented to the council for consideration on November 14, 1962, under the name "The Twofold Source of Revelation." The council as a whole did not accept the document well, and many severely criticized it because they felt that the schema did not adequately demonstrate the pastoral demands of the modern world, for which Pope John had called.

The debate continued until November 20, when a vote was taken to determine whether the schema as it stood was sufficient as a basis for further discussion or whether it should be redrafted by its preparatory commission. The vote fell short of the two-thirds needed to return it to its commission, but at this point, Pope John XXIII overrode that rule and formed a restructured commission to deal with the document.

This revised commission extensively rewrote the original draft. Overall, the commission used less philosophical language in its rewrite and more firmly rooted the document in Scripture and in the history of the Church. In keeping with Pius XII's encyclical, the document endorsed modern methods of biblical research. In the end, the schema dealt largely with Scripture. (Four out of six chapters deal with it directly and the remaining two are based upon it.)

When the final document was brought to a vote, the outcome was nearly unanimous: 2,344 to 6. Pope Paul VI promulgated the *Dogmatic Constitution on Divine Revelation* on November 18, 1965.

Neither the importance of this constitution nor its incompleteness can be overlooked. As the Church reforms itself in these times, and it must always be reformed, this document is an important milestone, but its full impact has not yet been felt.

Professional theologians rather than the members of the faithful, untrained in theology will be the ones who will finally realize the full impact of the *Dogmatic Constitution on Divine Revelation*. Nonetheless, the document belongs to all the faithful for they need to understand these matters more clearly and express insights loudly in the Church to allow the Holy Spirit to guide the Church on its way.

PART TWO: PARAPHRASE TEXT

*F*rom the Second Vatican Council
proclaimed by Pope Paul VI on November 18, 1965

Preface

1 The story of God's interaction with humankind

is an age-old mystery:
How does God speak to humanity?
How do we know that it is actually God whom we hear?
Is God really here,
    or is God's existence "wishful thinking"
    on our part?
Are the words of Scripture really God's words?

This council now wishes to address the matter
    of how God reveals Godself to humankind
    and how humans respond to the voice of God.
This we do in order to strengthen the faith of all people.
It is our hope that by hearing the message of Christ,
    all the world might believe,
    and, believing, might hope
    and, hoping, might love more profoundly.
In this, we take as our lead the words of St. John,
    expressed in the first letter,
    "What we have seen and heard
        we announce to you
        so that you may have community with us
        and together our community
            may be with God
            and God's Son, Jesus Christ."

Chapter One
REVELATION

2 God wants nothing less
    than that we come to know God fully:
    to know God's constant love,
    to understand God's unfathomable faithfulness,

to experience God right down to the marrow.
This is what we mean when we speak of revelation:
>   that we make plain and evident
>   the realities of God,
>>   who is so far above and beyond us,
>>   yet closer than our best friend.
Distinguishing the voice of God in the din of this world
>   is not usually easy for us,
>   yet that voice is as clear as the words "I do."
Indeed! Revelation is all that God wants to say to us,
>   whisper to us,
>   shout at us,
>   sing to us,
>   and breathe in us.

In revealing God's inner self,
>   God does not merely reveal information
>>   about the divine life,
>>   but invites us into close companionship.
God actually shares with us the divine nature
>   so that we are no longer strangers to God
>   or to one another.
God shows us what God is really like,
>   and in this process, we come to know God's heart
>   as God knows ours.
This activity of God revealing Godself to us
>   occurs with both words and deeds
>   which have an inner unity:
>>   The deeds of God in history
>>   confirm the teaching signified by the words
>>   while at the same time the words
>>>   proclaim the deeds
>>>   and interpret them for us!

Hence, the deepest truth about God shines out
    for all to see;
    indeed, our human connection with God
        is made known in Christ!
Christ is both the message and the messenger
    of all that God wants to say to us.

3 From the beginning, God has been with us,
    conscious of our human nature.
God continually promised us healing,
    by caring for us ceaselessly.
God was first manifest in creation,
    being known in wonder,
        power,
        majesty,
        and goodness
    through the created world.
Thus all people have access to God
    and all people can, on some level,
    come to know of God's existence and inner self.
Over the course of history, though,
    it has become more and more clear to us
    that God wishes to speak to us as friends,
        to live among us,
        and to invite us into close union.
God called Abraham and Sarah and their offspring
    to enter into friendship with God
    and later called Moses and Miriam
    and on through the prophets, . . .
        promising them divine closeness,
        promising them salvation.

4 And then there was the Christ!

God sent Jesus Christ to dwell with us
and to tell us about the inner life of God.
Jesus proclaimed through his life and death,
through his rising and remaining among us,
that God is indeed with us,
to free us from the darkness of sin
and to raise us up to life eternal.
Everything that God wanted to say to us for all eternity
was made known in Jesus Christ.
This was the perfect moment of divine revelation,
and we await nothing further:
no hidden secrets,
no sleight of hand,
no fine print.
Jesus Christ: today and for all eternity.
Nothing more,
nothing less.

5 Nor are we left here all alone.
The Holy Spirit brings all this to completion in us
by deepening our interior lives
so that this revelation might take root there.
Thus we are able to give free assent to these truths,
our hearts moved and turned toward God,
the eyes of our minds opened
by the Spirit.
6 Hence we can come to understand more fully
those divine matters and persons
which it is otherwise beyond us
to grasp!

Chapter Two
HANDING ON DIVINE REVELATION

7 We believe that God has made it possible
    for the revealed truths about our lives
    to be fully and faithfully handed on forever.
Jesus, therefore, sent his followers
    to announce this Good News,
    which they did in two ways.
    First, they preached and taught orally
        and observed a way of life
        based on Christ's teaching.
    Second, they eventually wrote down the message,
        under the guidance of the Spirit.
Then they handed on the authority to teach
    to the first bishops who took their place.
The role of those early bishops
    was to keep the entire message of Christ
        together,
        complete,
        and intact
    for all generations to know and understand.
8 We believe it is God's plan, then,
    that succeeding generations
    have access to the Word of God
    through an unending succession of preaching
        and witnessing
        until the end of time.
The message passed along in this way
    contains everything needed to live a holy life,
    and calls us to respond;
    we refer to our response as "faith."
This way of passing on the faith

is like passing on an inheritance
from one generation to the next.
  That which is most precious to the Church
  is lovingly guarded and, at the same time,
  generously and freely given
    to the daughters and sons of God.

Indeed, this "Deposit of Faith," this tradition,
  the Good News given by God,
  develops in the Church
  through the Holy Spirit.
Our Faith is not a static reality,
  lifeless and dead.
Rather, over time, there is growth in understanding
  and development in doctrine.
This growth and development occur
  through contemplation,
    study,
    and putting belief into action,
  producing a penetrating insight into faith.
Even the Scriptures themselves
  are more fully understood over time,
  each age hearing it as a living voice
    for that particular time.
[9] Hence, there is a very close connection
  between Scripture, on one hand,
  and Church tradition, on the other.

They both flow from the same divine well
  and tend toward the same goal.

Scripture is that written component of the Word of God,
  of which we have two volumes:
  Old Testament and New Testament.

Sacred tradition is the Word of God
    passed on to us in a variety of forms:
        Liturgy,
        prayers,
        teachings of the apostles,
        and truths not fully explained in Scripture
            but equally important.
We, therefore, honor both sources of knowledge:
    sacred Scripture and sacred tradition.
Both Scripture and tradition are essential components
    of the Word of God.

10 Today it is the task of the Church
    to keep the Word of God alive.
In all we say and all we do
    in our everyday lives,
        this Word of God grows more vibrant
        in the world.
Everyone who is baptized is empowered
    to understand the Word of God
    and to find meaning for their lives
        in this Word.
Bishops have a particularly important role
    in bringing the Word of God to light.
It is their role, in fact, to provide for authentic and uniform
    interpretation of the Word of God.
        By their consensus in this regard,
        they bring unity to the Church.
This is why our bishops are referred to collectively
    as "the magisterium,"
    which means "official teachers."

All bishops and others who teach the Word
    pass on only what is handed down to them.

They listen to the Word,
guard it carefully,
and explain it well,
all with the help of the Holy Spirit.
Thus, neither the Church as a whole
nor any teacher of the Church
is above the Word of God.

These three, then, are intimately linked:
Church tradition,
sacred Scripture,
and the magisterium of the Church.

Chapter Three
SACRED SCRIPTURE:
ITS DIVINE INSPIRATION AND INTERPRETATION

11 Those who wrote down the words of Scripture
were inspired by the Holy Spirit.
The Holy Spirit guided the writers
so that they recorded God's revelation to us.
At the same time, these writers
had full use of their intelligence,
their hearts,
their insights,
and access to their everyday experiences.
They were not mindless scribes,
unaware of what they were writing.
It is as though they were so in tune with the Holy Spirit
that everything they chose to write
was exactly what needed to be written.

Therefore, we believe that the books of Scripture
    teach solidly,
    faithfully,
    and without error
        everything that God wants them to teach.

12 However, those who read these words today
    must study them carefully
    in order to understand the original message of God.
It is, therefore, necessary for today's readers
    to investigate what the writers intended to say.
There are, for example, various forms of literature
    used in the Scriptures:
        historical,
        prophetic,
        poetic,
        and others.
In addition, there were circumstances
    in the days of the writers
    that differ from those in today's world and culture.
In order to understand the words of Scripture,
    one must understand these factors
    and how they influenced the text.
Not only that, we must also be careful to consider
    Scripture as a whole,
    not in fractions and broken parts.
13 The words of Scripture, after all,
    are human words
    imbued with the truth and holiness of God,
        and we must scrutinize them carefully
        to understand them fully.

Chapter Four
THE OLD TESTAMENT

14 God chose the people of Israel to form a sacred nation
    united by the covenant of love.
God revealed Godself
    so that the people of Israel
     could experience divine love
    and be a beacon of light to other nations.
As we have already said,
    God's revelation began among the Hebrew people
    when Abraham and Sarah were called forth.
God's Word was also made known through others,
    especially the prophets.
The books of the Old Testament preserve this memory
    of God's loving goodness to a people in slavery.
These books of the Old Testament
    remain permanently valuable
    because they show how God prepared the world
     to receive Christ.
15 They contain a store of marvelous teachings about God,
    wholesome wisdom about human life,
    and a wonderful treasury of prayers.
In all of this, the mystery of our salvation is present
    in a hidden way.
Christians should receive these books with reverence.
16 The two testaments are intimately linked,
    the new hidden in the old,
    and the old made manifest in the new.

Chapter Five
THE NEW TESTAMENT

17 Jesus Christ is Lord of heaven and earth!
He established himself as such
    in his works,
    his words,
    and his miracles.
Christ brought order
    to a world that was deep in chaos,
        frantic with fear,
        and starved for peace.
Thus, Christ established the Reign of God on earth.
Jesus showed us who God really is
    and completed God's work by dying
        and being raised.
The writings of the New Testament stand as God's witness
    to this marvelous reality.

18 Among the many books of Scripture,
    the Gospels have a special prominence.
They are our main way of knowing
    about the words and deeds of Christ.
The message they contain, in fact,
    is the foundation of our Faith.
There is really only one Gospel,
    the Gospel of Jesus Christ.
    But this one Gospel is given voice
        in four distinct books:
            Matthew,
            Mark,
            Luke,
            and John.

The message of the Gospels is the same message
    upon which the first apostles built their lives
    and founded the early Church.
This is the same faith
    for which many early Christians died.

[19] The Gospels are a written account
    of the stories and memories of Jesus.
And although they are not meant as historical records,
    what they contain is true:
        the story of the salvation of humankind
        and the truth about Jesus Christ.
[20] The letters of St. Paul
    and other apostolic writings
    are also contained in the New Testament,
        and all of them serve to more and more fully
        reveal the work of Christ.

Chapter Six
SACRED SCRIPTURE
IN THE LIFE OF THE CHURCH

[21] The Church venerates
    sacred Scripture and the Body of Christ
    with the same vigor.

Both of these are celebrated in our Liturgy.

The bread of life we are offered at Mass
    flows both from God's Word and from Christ's Body.
The altar around which we gather at Mass
    is really both the table of the Word of God

and the table of the Body of Christ.
All the teaching of the Church
    is nourished and focused, therefore,
    by sacred Scripture.
In Scripture, God meets us and speaks to us
    with great love.
The force and power of the Word of God
    is so great that it stands
    as the support and energy of the whole Church,
        the strength of faith for its members,
        the food of the soul,
        the pure source of the spiritual life.
22 Because this is true,
    easy access to Scripture should be provided
    to all the faithful.
Toward this end, new translations should be prepared
    in all the languages of the world.
Official translations of Scripture
    need to be approved by authorities at the Vatican
    in order to insure that they are authentic.
And we encourage cooperation
    among the various Christian Churches
    in preparing accurate translations of Scripture.

23–24 This council urges all who are preparing for ministry
    to be fully acquainted with Scripture.
The authentic study of theology rests,
    after all, on Scripture.
25 Indeed, all who work in the Church
    must be fully trained in the Scriptures
    and must use them as the basis of preaching,
        catechesis,
        and Christian instruction.
The faithful as well should know Scripture,

for through the words of these texts
   they meet Christ.
Even non-Christians should have access
   to sacred Scripture.

26 Just as the life of the Church is strengthened
   through more frequent celebration of the Eucharist,
   so it will be stimulated
      by a growing reverence for the Word of God
      which lasts forever.

The Constitution on the Sacred Liturgy
Sacrosanctum Concilium

Chapter Three

PART ONE: BACKGROUND

On the eve of Vatican II, two related movements were spreading throughout the world and taking firm hold on Catholic thinking, both in theological circles as well as in pastoral ones.

One was the liturgical movement, which had begun in the first decade of the century, taken hold in abbeys across Europe, moved into universities, spread with great force to North America, and included both serious scholarly work as well as experimentation with the rites.

The second was the biblical movement, which also had early beginnings, took firm hold in the Church, and had influence around the world.

These two movements, more than any others, could be cited as having given rise to the council itself. They might also be the reason why, in its second day of meetings on October 16, 1962, the council fathers selected the reform of the sacred Liturgy of the Church as its first task. As they considered their possible choices that day, the council fathers saw that, of the five possible first topics, only the schema on the Liturgy seemed to have the pastoral content and the reform-minded language that promised the *aggiornamento* on which Pope John had insisted.

As it was introduced for discussion at the council, the schema on the Liturgy contained within it a sound theology, based on principles tested over many years in the liturgical movement. The original schema on the Church had been prepared by a closed group of mainly conservative theologians in the Vatican. But the schema on the sacred Liturgy had emerged from a much more open process and group.

The preparatory commission on the Liturgy included (1) experts known for their wide backgrounds and (2) pastoral leaders from around the world. Indeed, nineteen nations were represented on this commission. In the ten years preceding Vatican II, there had been seven international liturgical conferences, the last of which occurred in Assisi, Italy, in 1956 with the enthusiastic blessing of Pope Pius XII. At this conference, the pope himself declared that the liturgical movement had proven itself to be, above all else, "a providential . . . movement of the Holy Spirit in His Church."

The schema presented to the council was truly the majority point of view. The conservative central commission had toned down the schema and reduced its suggested reforms in certain areas. But the council fathers, alerted to this, recharged the document with all its original plans for reform—and added more besides!

Theological experts had examined the schema which reached the floor of the council and had, wisely and intentionally, set it upon solid biblical ground. Various subcommittees of the preparatory commission spent four months writing and rewriting the schema, chapter by chapter, and the entire text was examined in detail by the commission itself no less than three times. No comma was unexamined; no line of Scripture accidentally chosen; no effort spared to produce a careful, solid document.

The debate on this schema began on October 22, 1962, and lasted until November 13. More than 325 council fathers spoke in general council sessions during that time. Later in the first session, when the schema on the Church was introduced and sent back for immediate revisions, some council fathers said that the document on the Church as presented by its preparatory commission was not in keeping with the foundations laid down during the debates on the sacred Liturgy.

Indeed, history has shown that the decision to work first on the reform of the Liturgy was a happy choice. Why? Because the document and the debate proved both to the skeptical world and to the world's bishops that the council would undertake true reform.

On November 14, 1962, only one month after convening in Rome, the Second Vatican Council approved the schema on the Liturgy *in principle* with an overwhelming vote of support. Only 46 council fathers voted no! Following this important vote, the council fathers considered amendments to the document, and about a year later, the council approved the final document by a vote of 2,147 to 4. Pope Paul VI promulgated it on December 4, 1963. It was the first council document passed and would have the most far-reaching effects in the lives of the faithful.

Catholics around the world began, after a pause of many centuries, to participate more fully in the rites of the Mass and other sacraments. They slowly put away their other devotional aides to focus on the Body of Christ and be "formed" by it. This has brought the council to the attention of average laypeople in a way that no debate on episcopal collegiality ever could have done!

Before we turn to the document itself, let's consider its main avenues of reform.

First and foremost, the document on the sacred Liturgy makes clear that the Church is indeed the whole People of God. It calls on this whole People to actively participate in the rites, taking new roles previously reserved to the clergy. This active, conscious, informed, and wholly new role for laypeople in the rites of the Mass and in the sacraments is surely what laid the groundwork for a sociological and psychological reunderstanding of themselves as Church. This newly emerging self-understanding of the Church as God's People is still unfolding. Evidence of this emerges as laypeople become more active ministers in both the Church and "the world," which is the Church's context.

The second main avenue of reform, which emerged from the liturgical movement and which received endorsement through the document on sacred Liturgy, is the restoration of baptism-linked-to-confirmation as the essential and basic sacrament of ministry. The renewed emphasis on baptism shifts the focus of ministry in the Church. Where once ministry was seen as belonging solely to the ordained, now the council was declaring that it belongs, indeed, to all the baptized. The full impact of this shift will take many years to understand and unfold.

A third avenue of reform is the recognition that local parishes and dioceses actually do constitute a full expression of the Church, rather than mere geographic divisions. This has reversed an understanding that had been in place since the Church became the government of Europe at the fall of the Roman Empire. Because of all the reformed thinking of the council fathers, the document allows for and encourages the use of appropriate local customs and languages in the celebration of the rites; it provides for cultural adaptation. Indeed, how else can the Church ever achieve the full and active participation of the faithful?

A final avenue of reform which the *Constitution on the Sacred Liturgy* traveled down is its basis in Scripture. This council document may well be the one most closely influenced by the modern biblical movement. The document roots its reforms in the Paschal Mystery and in the theology of the Church expressed in the letters of the apostles. The document also calls emphatically for the restoration of a wider use of Scripture in the Liturgy of the Word, for preaching based on Scripture, and for courses on Scripture for seminarians and laypeople alike. From the First Letter of Peter, where Christians are called a "chosen race and a royal priesthood," to the First Letter to the Corinthians, which says that Christians, "though many, are one body because [they] partake of the one bread," the texts of sacred Scripture form the basis of the reformed thinking in the document on sacred Liturgy, helping to make the reforms solid, ecumenical, and lasting.

PART TWO: PARAPHRASE TEXT

*F*rom the Second Vatican Council
proclaimed by Pope Paul VI on December 4, 1963

Introduction

1 We who are the participants in this,
      the Second Vatican Council,
      have a sense of both hope and urgency
            for the Church.
We desire much for the world
      and believe that the Church
      has much to offer to all people.
Therefore, in all the work that is set out before us,
      we intend to adhere to
            the following ideals:
First, Christian life is to be lived with vigor.
      Our hope is that through the reform of this council,

Christians may embrace the Christian faith
    more profoundly each day.
Second, our world has changed substantially in recent years.
    Where it is both possible and beneficial,
    we want the Church to change as well
    in order to more graciously serve
    the needs of our day.
Third, presently, Christians are not fully united.
    We want to nurture and promote everything
    that will help to bring about greater understanding
    and more authentic unity
        among all Christian people.
Fourth, the Church has much to offer humankind.
    We want to strengthen those elements of the Church
    that allow people to experience
    the deep love of God
    and the challenging call of Christ.
Given these ideals
    and the reform that is already happening
    in the Church,
    we believe that now is the right time
        to bring about reform
            in the way we worship and pray.
We therefore want to reform the Liturgy
    and increase our fervor for it.

2 The essential work of redemption
    is accomplished mainly through the Liturgy,
    especially the Eucharist.
This is true because it is through participation in the Liturgy
    that we are given everything that we need
    to understand the mystery
        of our relationship with Christ.
We are given the strength we need

to witness to the reality of Christ in our lives
and in the life of the Church.
3 Christ is intimately knowable
and is at the same time a mystery.
Hence, the Church is also at the same time
both understandable and incomprehensible.
The Church is both human and divine,
visible and invisible,
eager to act and intent on contemplation,
present in the world
yet not fully at home here.
The Liturgy helps us to live with this tension
and thus enter fully into a life of faith.
It is the Liturgy that builds up those who are present
and is also a sign to those who are not.
The Liturgy is an expression of our life in the Spirit
and a sign to the world of ultimate unity.
It enables those who participate
to reach full and conscious Christian maturity.
4 We are, therefore, setting forth some ideals
under which the Liturgy should be reformed
and by which it can be embraced fully
by the faithful.
We intend to outline the essential principles of Liturgy,
which should always be followed.
We will also establish some practical norms,
which are intended to be applied
to specific cases.
The rites of the Catholic Church hold a particular dignity,
and we want to preserve them.
We also want to revise these rites
so that, when celebrated with greater vigor,
they will be better able to address
the circumstances of modern times.

Chapter One
General Principles for Restoration
and Promotion of the Sacred Liturgy

5 We know that time has its way
of stopping for no one.
Creeping by at a snail's pace or thundering through our lives
like a runaway locomotive,
time is always lost, never gained.
And in this sense, time will always disappoint.
Yet far beneath the surface of time,
there runs a deep river,
eternity.
Sometimes we get a taste of this river
as it bubbles forth
like a spring of living water.
In those moments, time seems wedded to eternity.
The whole world and we along with it
know that, yes, everything is in the hand of God.
Long ago, such a moment occurred.
It remains forever within our grasp.
Time burst at the seams,
and the eternal Reign of God gushed forth:
The fullness of time!
Jesus Christ!
Such was the coming of the Anointed One.
So tangible was eternity in the person of Jesus
that those who encountered him
found themselves completely healed,
fully forgiven,
and totally united with God,
with each other,
and even with their own very selves.
It was as though they had crossed the threshold of eternity:

no longer slaves to the disappointments of time
but free to discover at every moment
the thread of eternity which holds all of life together.
They found that in this community of believers
there existed a new way of being in the world.
Freely reconciled in Christ, they were thus free to bring
their entire selves to the throne of God
and worship God in absolute humility
and dignity.
All that Jesus gave to the human race
was principally achieved
through the Paschal Mystery.
When we speak of the Paschal Mystery,
we refer to Jesus' profound death,
burial,
resurrection,
and sending of the apostles to the world.
The Gospel of John gives us a vivid image
of the magnitude of this Paschal Mystery.
The Gospel writer tells how a spear was driven
deep into Christ's heart
as he waited upon the cross.
From this noble heart,
God's very life gushed forth upon the world:
eternity!
Christ's life drenched the whole earth
that Friday afternoon.
And like a soft rain,
it gave new life to the parched soil
of humanity's heart.
This, we might say, is really when the Church was born.

6 For Christ did not pour out his life for us
just to leave us abandoned.

Instead, Christ sent the Holy Spirit
　　to fill the lives of the first apostles and disciples
　　and to stir up in them
　　the desire to live fully at the table
　　　　of God's gracious love.
Thus the first followers of Jesus
　　were empowered to preach the Good News.
And God also gave to those first disciples
　　everything that they needed
　　to remain fully attentive
　　to the mystery that they had experienced
　　during Christ's life on earth.
Thus did they baptize those who came to believe
　　in Christ and in the saving power
　　of his life and death.
Thus, too, did they share together the Eucharist,
　　the full celebration of the presence of Christ.
It was both in their loving actions
　　and in their worship
　　that the first disciples came to know
　　　　their profound call to "be Church."
From that very first day until now,
　　we have never stopped announcing the Word,
　　　　baptizing those who believe,
　　　　and celebrating the Eucharist
　　　　　　as God's priestly people.
The early writings of Christians,
　　contained mainly in our Bible,
　　demonstrate this clearly.
The second chapter of Acts of the Apostles
　　tells explicitly how those who
　　believed the words of St. Peter were baptized.
They also continued steadfastly, the text tells us,
　　"in the communion of the breaking of bread

and in prayers."
So today we continue in this holy tradition,
    holding out hope that by doing so,
    we, too, will come to know the presence of Christ.

7 We have lost nothing
    for not having lived during the time
    of Jesus' life on earth.
We have everything that the first disciples had
    to help us believe in Jesus
    and live as though this faith
        really makes a difference!
Yet that is exactly what Christ promised;
    and being faithful to that promise,
        Christ is always present in the Church.
This presence is most noticeable
    in our liturgical celebrations.
In the Mass Christ is really present
    in the minister,
    in the eucharistic bread and wine,
    in the proclaimed Word of God,
    and in the whole community
        gathered to worship and pray.
Christ is also present in a special way
    in all the other sacraments.
Because of Christ's assured presence,
    the Liturgy gives us the unique opportunity
        to enter fully and honestly into
        our most right and authentic relationship
            with God.
Hence, the Liturgy is the most sacred act of human life.
    Nothing more significant is ever done.

8 The Liturgy is really a celebration of eternity,

here and now.
It contains the entire mystery of faith:
    it is our food as pilgrims,
    our hymn of praise,
    our hope for partnership with God.
The sacred Liturgy gathers together
    all who have gone before us
    and all who will come after us
        together with Jesus Christ,
        the Alpha and the Omega.
9 But even though Liturgy is most essential to us,
    it is not all we do as members of the Church.
Various ministries and activities of the Church
    help to give witness to the truth of Christ's presence
    in the whole world.
The ministry of preaching and teaching
    helps those who have not yet heard the Word of God
    to experience the first stirring of faith
        and the pull of eternity at their hearts.
Preaching and teaching also helps
    those who already follow Christ
    to grasp more firmly and clearly
    the mysteries of the faith they are trying to live.
Other ministries of service and compassion
    within both the Church and the world
    show clearly the call of the Christian
        to be the Light of the World.

10 Nevertheless, the Liturgy is the summit toward which
    the Christian life is directed
    and the very source of that life to begin with.
It is a fount from which grace is poured over us,
    and it is that place to which we go
        for reconciliation,

peace,
and communion.
Among all liturgical celebrations,
the Eucharist, of course, holds a special prominence.
In the Eucharist, the eternal covenant
between God and humankind is renewed
and Christ's love is rekindled in us.

11 Precisely because it is so central to us,
and so important in the Christian journey,
the faithful who come to Liturgy
must be well disposed,
ready to participate,
and actively engaged in the rites.
It is not enough simply to follow the letter of the law,
making sure that our liturgies
are "correct" and "proper."
Much more is required of those
who practice liturgical leadership:
it is also their duty to ensure that participants
have the opportunity
to take part fully,
to understand what they are doing,
and to be enriched by its effects.
12 We do realize that participating in the Liturgy
is not all that is required for the spiritual life.
There is also the need for private prayer
and witness to the life-giving death of Jesus.

13 Therefore, popular devotions and all practices
that help to foster a richer
and more authentic faith life
are encouraged.
Such devotions, however, should be in harmony

with the liturgical season
and always draw people more deeply
into the celebration of sacred Liturgy.
14 Because of their baptisms,
all the faithful have both a right and a duty
to full and active participation in the Liturgy.
Participation in the Liturgy can be seen as a "right"
because without it a person would experience
spiritual starvation.
It is a "duty" because without the Liturgy,
Christian people cannot live the life
to which God calls them.
In this sense, Liturgy is as basic as food and clothing:
everyone has a right to life's basic necessities,
and all people have an obligation
to care for their own bodies.
Therefore, we, the participants
in this Second Vatican Council,
propose one guiding principle before all others
as we approach the question on restoring
and reforming the sacred Liturgy.
The principle is this:
In the restoration and promotion of the sacred Liturgy,
the full and active participation by all the people
is the aim to be considered
before all else!
We realize that if the ideal
of full and active participation by all people
is ever to be realized,
then liturgical leaders, particularly pastors,
must be absolutely and internally convinced
of the spirit and power
of the Liturgy.
In this way they can pass on such fervor

to all the faithful entrusted to their ministry.

[15] Therefore, professors appointed to teach in seminaries
and institutes of pastoral education
must be properly trained.

[16] In seminaries, the study of Liturgy
is to be ranked among the compulsory courses.
The Liturgy in all its dimensions,
theological,
historical,
spiritual,
practical,
and legal,
is to be fully explored.
All seminary course work is to connect itself to Liturgy.

[17] Seminarians are also required to be formed
in liturgical piety,
celebrating the mysteries
and observing the liturgical year.

[18] Those priests already working in the field
are to be offered training now.

[19] And all the faithful should likewise be offered updating,
taking into account their age and condition,
their way of life and religious culture,
so they may become active participants.

[20] The use of the media to transmit the rites
should be done with discretion and dignity.

[21] So that the faithful may more certainly derive
an abundance of graces,
the Church now undertakes a general restoration
of the sacred Liturgy.
The Liturgy is composed of elements
that cannot be changed.
But among these have crept in

other elements that are out of harmony
　　with the inner nature of the Liturgy
　.　and are, therefore, unsuited for it.
We are restoring both texts and rites
　　so they more clearly express the holy things
　　that they signify.

22 As we begin to move toward restoration of the Liturgy,
　　we pause to remind all
　　that the regulation of the Liturgy
　　　　is the proper work of the pope
　　　　and sometimes also the local bishop.
Within certain defined limits, the regulation of the Liturgy
　　belongs also to various local bodies of bishops
　　who set forth norms for their regions.
　　　　Others should not make changes.
23 When implementing change,
　　consider carefully and first
　　any theological, historical, or pastoral aspects of it.
Take into account recent experiences,
　　recent liturgical norms,
　　and the good of the Church.
In most cases, reforms should grow from existing customs;
　　care should be taken that great differences in style
　　do not exist within a single region.

24 The Scriptures are of greatest importance
　　to the liturgical celebration,
　　so care should be taken in proclaiming them,
　　　　homilizing on them,
　　　　singing hymns derived from them,
　　　　or praying inspired by them.
A warm and living love of the Scriptures
　　is to be fostered.

25 The liturgical books are to be revised
    as soon as possible,
    employing experts and consulting the bishops.
26 We are reminded that liturgical services
    are not private functions
    but celebrations of the whole Church.
27 So whenever rites have a communal nature,
    they should be set in a communal setting,
        not in a private one.
This is especially true of the Mass and the sacraments.

28 Anyone with a part of the rite to perform
    should do all of, but only,
    that which pertains to his or her role.
29 Servers, lectors, commentators, and members of the choir
    exercise a genuine liturgical function
    and should do so with piety and decorum.
They must, therefore, be well trained.

30 The laypeople should take an active role as well
    by acclamations, responses, songs, and actions,
    as well as by their posture.
At the proper times,
    a reverent silence should be observed.
31 As the liturgical books are revised,
    the people's parts should be included.
32 The Liturgy makes clear who has what role,
    as well as the place of the ordained,
    and allows for the recognition of civil authorities,
        but no special honors are to be paid
        in the Liturgy to private persons or classes.
33 The sacred Liturgy is both worship of God
    as well as instruction for the faithful.
In the Liturgy, God speaks to the people

and Christ proclaims the Good News.
The people reply to God
    in both song and prayer.
34 Therefore, the rites should be distinguished
    by a noble simplicity;
      they should be short, clear,
        and unencumbered by repetitions.
Explanation of their meaning should not be necessary.

35 There is to be more reading from Scripture,
    with more variance and suitability.
Sermons should be drawn mainly from Scripture
    and should proclaim God's wonderful works,
      the mystery of Christ,
      and the wonderful moment
        that we share together at Mass.
Liturgical instruction itself should be brief
    and should not intrude on the rites.
Bible services are encouraged,
    especially on vigils or when no priest is present.

36 The use of Latin is preserved
    but the use of the mother tongue,
    which may be of great advantage to the people,
      is also permitted
      when requested by the local bishops.
Translations into the mother tongue must be approved.

37 The Church does not wish to impose
    a rigid uniformity
    in matters where it is not necessary,
    and local customs may be introduced into the Liturgy
      provided they are not based in superstition
        or error.

38 Therefore, provisions for adaptations of this sort
   shall be made.
39 Such adaptations for different groups,
   regions,
   and peoples
      shall be drawn up
      and approved by the local bishops.
40 When more extensive adaptations are needed,
   they should likewise be carefully studied
      and approved.
41 The local bishop is essentially the "high priest"
   of the diocese, and with the local priests,
   they form one priesthood
   with the full active participation of the people.
42 But because it is impossible
   for a diocese of one parish to exist,
   pastors take the place of the bishop
   and the liturgical life of the parish is to be fostered
      above all else.
Such parishes constitute a full expression of the Church
   and are not mere geographic divisions.

43 We hereby call for all to enter into
      the promotion and restoration of the Liturgy
         with zeal!
44 Toward this end, liturgical commissions
   are to be established wherever they will foster
   vigorous pastoral-liturgical action,
      especially in local dioceses,
         groups of dioceses,
         and parishes.
45 These commissions are to
   regulate pastoral-liturgical action,
   promote study,

and experiment appropriately
in reforming
and implementing approved rites.
46 Likewise there are to be formed commissions
on sacred music
and sacred art,
working in tandem and close cooperation
with the liturgical commission.

Chapter Two
THE MOST SACRED MYSTERY OF THE EUCHARIST

47 Christ instituted the eucharistic celebration
at his last supper with his friends.
His purpose was to provide the Church
with a memorial of his loving death and resurrection:
a sacrament of love,
a sign of unbreakable unity,
a bond of charity and justice,
all filling us with grace.
48 The Church wants the faithful, therefore,
to find Christ present at the Eucharist.
We're not present at Mass merely as strangers
or as silent spectators,
but we are to take an active part in the rites,
and understand what we're doing.
49 For this reason, we participants in Vatican II,
having in mind mainly those Masses
where the faithful are present,
call for revision of the rites
to make Liturgy more effective for all.
50 The rites of the Mass are, therefore, to be revised

in such a way that their real purpose is served
and the active participation of the faithful
   will be increased.
The rites are to be simplified,
   duplications are to be eliminated,
   and elements added with little advantage
      are to be discarded.
Other elements that have suffered injury over time
   are to be restored to the vigor they had
   during the days of the holy Fathers and Mothers
      or as may seem useful or necessary.

51 The treasures of the Bible are to be opened up
   and a more representative portion of them read
   so that a richer fare may be provided
      at the table of God's Word.

52 The homily should reflect on the mysteries of the faith,
   suggested by the rites or readings,
   and should not be omitted except rarely.

53 The prayer of the faithful,
   following the homily,
   is to be restored, and the people are to take part,
      praying for the whole Church,
      the civil society,
      and other needs.

54 The mother tongue may be used when suitable,
   but Latin should be retained for those parts
      where it fits best.

55 The faithful should receive communion at Mass,
   and permission for communion under both kinds
   is granted at the discretion of the local bishops.

56 The two parts of the Mass,
   the Liturgy of the Word
   and that of the Eucharist,
      are tightly linked

and people should take part
in the entire celebration.
57 Concelebration, where two or more priests or bishops
celebrate with one another and the people,
is to be restored for certain times and places.
58 A new rite for concelebration should be drawn up.

Chapter Three
OTHER SACRAMENTS AND THE SACRAMENTALS

59 The purpose of the sacraments
is to encourage holiness among people,
to build up the Body of Christ,
and to give worship to God.
They are signs that also instruct.
They presuppose faith,
but they also nourish,
strengthen,
and express it.
They are sources of grace,
but also, the very act of celebrating them
assists the faithful in receiving grace effectively.
Because they are so important,
everyone should understand them well.

60 The Church has also instituted sacramentals,
sacred signs that bear a resemblance
to sacraments.
61 All this is meant to incorporate people's whole lives
into the power of God.
62 But over time, there have crept into these sacred rites
certain features that have rendered their nature

unclear.
We wish to reform them as well at this council.

63 The mother tongue can be used more widely
in celebrating the sacraments.
The rites are to be reformed and adapted to these times,
taking into account the needs of different regions.
64 The catechumenate for adults is to be restored
and appropriate rites developed
to provide for initiation of the participants.
65 Elements of initiation rites already in use in mission lands
are permitted when they can be suitably adapted
for Christian use.

66 The rite for the baptism of adults is to be revised,
taking into account its place in the catechumenate.
67 Likewise, the rite for the baptism of infants
is to be revised,
emphasizing more the role of parents
and godparents.
68 These rites are to contain variants,
to be used with local discretion,
including some for use by catechists
in mission lands.
69 A new rite is also to be devised for those already baptized
celebrating their entry into full communion
with the Catholic Church.
70 Except during Eastertide,
baptismal water may be blessed
within the rite of baptism,
using a shorter formula.
71 Confirmation rites are to be revised
with an emphasis on its connection to baptism;
they should, in fact, include a renewal

of baptismal promises.

72 The rite and formula for the sacrament of penance
    is to be revised
    to better emphasize the nature of the sacrament
        with its focus on the mercy of God.

73–75 "Extreme unction" will be called
    "anointing of the sick,"
    and its rites and prayers are to be revised
    for use at times other than the point of death.

76 The rites and texts for the ordination of priests
    are to be revised.

77–78 The rites for marriage are to be revised
    and may include suitable local customs.
In all cases, the priest must ask for and obtain
    the consent of the parties.
It should normally be celebrated within the Mass,
    with the prayer for the bride amended
    to remind both parties of their equal obligation
        to remain faithful to each other.

79 Sacramentals are to undergo a revision
    that takes into account the principle
    of active, intelligent participation by the faithful.
Some may be administered by laypeople.

80 The rites for the consecration of virgins
    and for religious profession and renewal
    should be drawn up to achieve greater dignity.

81 The rite for burial of the dead

should express more clearly the connection
to Christ's death and rising
and should take into account customs found
in various regions.
82 Finally, the rite for the burial of children
should be revised,
and a special Mass provided for the occasion.

Chapter Four
THE DIVINE OFFICE

83 The work of Christ is a song of praise for God,
and the Church now continues that hymn
by celebrating the Eucharist
but also by praying the divine office.
84 An ancient tradition of the Church,
the divine office is composed in such a way
that all the hours of day and night
are filled with prayer.
This is the very prayer of the Body of Christ!
85 Therefore, those who pray this holy office
have the special honor of representing
the whole Church
standing before God in praise daily.
86 Prayer and the ministry of the Word
were tightly linked by the early followers of Christ
whose example we now take.
87 But in order to make this more powerful
and a greater benefit to all who pray it,
the council wishes to enact certain reforms.
88 First and foremost, the prayer will be reorganized
so that the prayers are genuinely related

to the hour of day
at which they are prayed.
We will also take into account
the modern conditions of apostolic ministry
and how daily life is lived in these times.
89 We declare first, therefore,
that Lauds as morning prayer and
Vespers as evening prayer
are the two hinges on which the office turns.
These are the chief hours
and should be observed as such.
Compline will be revised as a suitable evening prayer
for the end of day.
The other hours of prayer will be revised as well.
90–94 Those who pray the office
should attune their minds and hearts to the prayer,
and revisions should make this more possible,
including revision of the readings,
the hymns,
the length of the Psalter,
and the time of day.
95–97 Communities are bound to celebrate the office daily
as are clerics not in community,
except when a liturgical service may substitute,
at the discretion of the local bishop.
98–100 Members of religious institutes whose constitutions
obligate them to pray specific parts of the office,
as well as priests living in common
who pray together,
are expressing the praise of the Church
when they pray.
Laypeople, too, are encouraged to pray the divine office
with local priests,
among themselves,

or even individually.

101 Latin is to be retained for the office,
  but the local bishop may allow the mother tongue
  when the use of Latin
      is an obstacle to understanding.

Chapter Five
THE LITURGICAL YEAR

102 The Church unfolds its celebrations of the mysteries
  of the faith
  in an annual calendar,
      observing Sundays each week
      as well as a cycle of feasts from Christmas
          to Pentecost.

103–5 In so doing, we honor Mary with special devotion,
  as well as the memory of the martyrs
      and other saints
  along with seasons of traditional disciplines.

106 Sunday is the original feast day
  and is a day when the faithful come together
      in one place.
The faithful should develop Sunday as a time of joy
  and freedom from work.
      In fact, Sunday and its liturgical celebration
          are to be a focus of church life.

107–8 The calendar of the liturgical year is to be revised
  in such a way that the feasts of the Lord
  take precedence over all others.
The sacred seasons of Advent-Christmastide
  and Lent-Eastertide
  should be emphasized to nourish the faithful.

109–10 The season of Lent is both
    a time of preparation for baptism
    and a time of penance for the faithful,
    in both cases to prepare us for the feast of Easter.
Hence, the practice of penance should be fostered
    in ways that suit our times
        and the local region.
111 We should continue to observe the feasts of the saints,
    but more of them should be confined
    to local regions.

Chapter Six
SACRED MUSIC

112 The Church has a great treasure in its music,
    more so than any other art,
    because sacred song united to the words
    forms a necessary part of the solemn Liturgy.
113–14 Liturgical worship is more noble
    when sung,
    hence choirs must be promoted,
        but all the faithful should also sing
        as part of the active participation
        we have called for here.
115 Music is to be taught in all seminaries
    and houses of formation.
116 While the Church considers Gregorian chant
    especially well suited for the Liturgy,
    it likewise admits other forms of music,
        especially polyphony.
117 An edition of a Gregorian chant hymnal
    for use in smaller parishes

should be prepared.

118–19 Singing by the people should be fostered,
and local musical traditions should be welcomed
when suitable.

120 In the Roman Catholic Church, the pipe organ
is to be held in high esteem,
but other instruments may be used
provided they are dignified
and truly contribute to the edification
of the faithful.

121 Composers should be encouraged,
and they should draw the words for their music
principally from holy Scripture
and liturgical sources.

Chapter Seven
SACRED ART AND FURNISHINGS

122 The Church has a long tradition of appreciating
and incorporating fine arts into its worship spaces
because by their very nature
such works give praise to God.

123 As such, we admit all kinds of art,
taking no one particular style as our own,
provided that what is chosen is dignified
and edifying.

124 And whether in selecting and retaining art
or sacred vessels and vestments,
pastors should strive after noble beauty
rather than sumptuous display.

125 When new churches are built, care should be taken
that they are suitable for liturgical celebrations

including the participation of the faithful.
Placing sacred images in churches may be continued,
    but their number should be moderate
    and their relative placement in right order.
126–27 Bishops and pastors should consult their
    commission on sacred art when making selections,
    and bishops should take special care of artists,
    to imbue them with the spirit of the sacred.
128 Along with the revisions of the liturgical books,
    there is to be an early revision of the statutes
    that govern material things involved with worship.
Local bishops are empowered
    to make most of these determinations.
129 Seminarians are to be taught about sacred art,
    its history and meaning,
    so they, too, will assist in its preservation.

*The Pastoral Constitution
on the Church
in the Modern World*

Gaudium et Spes

Chapter Four

PART ONE: BACKGROUND

*D*uring the preparatory period in advance of the council, no one made plans to include the constitution on the Church's relationship to the modern world as one of the council's documents. Indeed, no previous council in the entire history of the Church had done so. The idea for this document arose, instead, among the council fathers themselves and was given birth from the council floor itself!

One of the things that makes the *Pastoral Constitution on the Church in the Modern World* so unique is that never before has a church council addressed itself to all humankind without insisting that all the readers be baptized or give their allegiance to Rome! The document seeks to befriend and engage people of goodwill everywhere to make human life on this planet more dignified and, hence, closer to God's plan for us humans.

Gaudium et Spes is truly an international, transglobal, ecumenical document summarizing what we humans believe about ourselves. It might be argued that this is the first time in our history when we humans have reflected together so profoundly on the very nature of our humanness and drawn out of that a statement of our common beliefs.

Having done this, the *Pastoral Constitution on the Church in the Modern World* hopes that we will now proceed with richer relationships among ourselves, more economic justice, less threat of war, a more humane use of technology, and a generally more noble lifestyle for all people.

Perhaps this document will be only one of many that will engage all humanity in dialogue.

Significantly, in the midst of the debate on this document, Pope Paul VI became the first pope in history to address the United Nations in person. His oral message to the world given in New York City and this written one prepared at the council in Rome, from which he departed and to which he returned, are synonymous.

Many factors at Vatican II gave rise to this document: Pope John's opening speech calling for optimism, the role of the Church in the world, the vision of the Church as the People of God, the inclusion of all people of goodwill in the council's opening message, and the strong accommodation to the values of ecumenism.

But the more immediate stimulus was a speech on December 4, 1962, by a Belgian cardinal, Leon-Josef Suenens. As Vatican I was the council of the papacy, he said, let this be the council of the Church of Christ who is the Light of the Nations! He went on to propose that the schema on the nature of the Church (which Cardinal Ottaviani's commission had presented) be divided into two parts, one dealing with the inner nature of the Church as the Mystical Body and the other with the Church's mission in the world.

Suenens called on the council to dialogue with the society around it on matters such as the dignity of the human person, social justice, private property, the poor, internal peace within nations, and international relations.

His speech that day was met with so much sustained applause that the day's president had to choke it off with a firm reminder that such boisterous responses were not in order!

In the following days, as debate on whether to accept the original schema on the Church moved toward a call for major revisions, others joined Suenens in his idea. Among them was Cardinal Augustin Bea, Cardinal Giacomo Lercaro, and most significantly, Cardinal Giovanni Battista Montini of Milan.

Cardinal Montini (who was one of the only cardinals invited to be a house guest of Pope John during the first council session in the fall and early winter of 1962) spoke only twice at the first session of the council. In this speech, he said he approved of Cardinal Suenens's remarks completely, confirming in the council that Suenens had indeed been speaking the mind of the pope.

Montini went on to say that the Church is nothing by itself. It is not so much that the Church has Christ, he said, but that Christ has the Church to carry on his work of bringing salvation to all. (Only a few months later, Cardinal Montini was elected to the papacy and chose the name Paul VI.)

Even though this clarion call for a second document arose from the floor of the council itself with the acclamation of the assembly and the blessing of the pope, actual work on it got under way slowly. Why? Because the commissions were busy with other work and because the writers were not exactly sure about how to proceed. Thus, other work took precedence in the council until the schema was finally presented on October 20, 1964.

Work on this document had proceeded in Rome as well as in Belgium, Geneva, and other locations convenient for committee meetings. The first drafts were in French, rather than Latin, a departure from the norm. Indeed, how could a document address the needs of the "modern world" in a language not considered modern for many centuries? (The schema was later translated into Latin for final debate and promulgation.)

Following the schema's presentation to the council for debate on October 20, 1964, many council fathers still considered it unworthy of council action because the schema sounded "unchurchy" to them. It was too "social" for many to take seriously. But debate on the council floor eventually convinced nearly everyone of the schema's worthiness. (Reporting the entire debate from St. Peter's to a waiting world, the press greeted the document with mounting interest.)

During the course of the debate, the council fathers formed a subcommittee to pay special attention to the schema's doctrinal soundness and its fidelity to biblical understandings. Another subcommittee spent time reflecting on the "signs of the times," a notion expressed first by Pope John XXIII. This second committee wanted the document to be truly universal and to address the signs of the times across the planet and not only in the Western world.

Bishops from around the world, along with various theological experts, sat on these subcommittees and between them they had an enormous influence on corrections to the document before the final votes were called for. Father Bernard Häring, the secretary of the commission, worked closely with Father Haubtmann of Paris, who drafted the text itself.

Over its months of editing, the schema grew in length and complexity, and the council fathers finally approved it as a basis for discussion, although there were many speeches and many recommendations for amendments.

From January 31 to February 6, 1965, a working group consisting of twenty-nine council fathers along with other experts met outside Rome to incorporate the suggested amendments and to check for doctrinal, biblical, and ecumenical needs in the document. This group met again from March 29 to April 6 that year. The group made an enormous effort to produce a workable, readable document, faithful to the Church and helpful to the world. (The working sessions required eighteen-hour days from many who were present!)

Nonetheless, as this document was debated in the fourth year of Vatican II, many further revisions were still called for. Repetitions were eliminated, incoherences examined, texts made shorter or longer, biblical references clarified, and language sought that would fairly and adequately express the mind of today's people. In the council vote during which suggestions could be made, thousands of amendments were proposed! When so much other work was also on the docket for the next two months, how could the council consider and debate all these amendments and get the texts rewritten to accommodate them?

But the work proceeded with both care and haste, deadlines were kept, and the document was completed in time for its final vote on December 7, 1965. The council fathers approved it by a vote of 2,309 to 75.

If any of the council documents call for midrash, this one does. It bears repeated study and reading. In fact, to gain the full development of the thought presented in the *Pastoral Constitution on the Church in the Modern World*, one ought to return frequently to the original translated language of the document itself.

Of course, in the years since the council ended, new challenges have arisen that the human family must face and new questions have forced themselves upon us. No single document could ever hope to address all of these. But midrash on the principles articulated in the *Pastoral Constitution on the Church in the Modern World* can lead us to deeper dialogue with each other as we humans move into our future together.

PART TWO: PARAPHRASE TEXT

*F*rom the Second Vatican Council
proclaimed by Pope Paul VI on December 8, 1965

Preface

[1] "The joy and hope, the grief and anxiety
    of the people of this age,
    especially those who are poor
    or in any way afflicted:
        this is the joy and hope,
            the grief and anxiety,
            of the followers of Christ."
Indeed, nothing genuinely human
    fails to raise an echo in their hearts.
The Christian community
    is, after all, a community of women and men
    truly linked with humankind and its history,
        bearing a message of salvation
        intended for all people.
[2] This council, therefore,
    having already looked in depth at the Church itself,
    now turns its attention on the whole of humanity.
We want to state clearly our understanding
    of the presence and function of the Church
    in the world of today.
For the world is the theater of human history,
    its energies,
    its tragedies,
    and its triumphs.

The Christian vision is that the world was created
    and is sustained
        by God.
It was freed from the slavery of sin by Christ.
It is now being re-created and brought to its destiny
    under the Holy Spirit.
3 We now offer to the world
    the honest assistance of the Church
    in fostering human harmony which is our destiny.
In this, we follow our teacher, Christ,
    who came to give witness to truth
        and to serve and not be served.
People today are troubled and perplexed
    by questions about their lives in the world,
    about their place in the universe,
    about the meaning of individual and collective work,
        and about the purpose and nature
        of being human.
We now wish to enter into dialogue
    with the whole human family about all this.
We will clarify these questions
    in the light of the Gospel
    and offer the human race the saving resources
        of the Church.
Our entire subject is humankind,
    men and women:
        whole and entire
        with body and soul,
        with heart and conscience,
        with mind and will.

Introductory Statement

4 In order to proceed here,
    we must understand the world in which we live,
        its expectations,
        its longings,
            and its often dramatic ways.
In language understandable for each generation,
    the Church should be able to give
    a meaningful answer to questions people have
        about life:
        both now and after death.
We must, in other words, read the signs of the times.

One of those signs
    is the profound and rapid change
    that is everywhere.
Riding on the intelligence of the human race,
    the creative energies of people
    have produced unprecedented social transformation.
As we might expect,
    this transformation has also brought
        serious difficulties.
Never has the human race enjoyed more wealth,
    yet a huge number of people are tormented
        by poverty, illiteracy, and want.
Never has there been such human freedom in the world,
    yet new forms of social and psychological slavery
        also make their appearance alongside it.
Never has the world been so close to the brink of unity
    and interdependence,
    yet new and opposing camps
        threaten this possibility.
There is even the frightening prospect

of a war of total destruction!
Never before has the drive for a better world
    been more on the minds of men and women,
        yet there is not a corresponding spiritual advancement
            to give it meaning and guidance.
As a result, many people are burdened with uneasiness
    even as they enjoy the benefits
        of modern life.
We humans must respond to all of this;
    indeed, we cannot escape doing so.

5 Today's spiritual hungers result, in part,
    from a much more scientific approach
    to understanding the world.
Technology is transforming the world,
    not to mention outer space!
And to a certain extent, the human intellect
    is even beginning to control time:
        the past by means of historical knowledge,
        the future by means
            of projecting and planning.
Likewise, advances in the social sciences,
    including biology, psychology, and others,
    bring us hope of improved self-knowledge.
At the same time,
    the human race is now considering the regulation
    of its own population growth.
History speeds along on so rapid a course
    that one can scarcely keep abreast of it,
    and we humans have now passed
        from a rather static understanding of reality
        to one much more dynamic
            and evolutionary!
6 By this very fact, local groups,

such as families, clans, or villages,
are rapidly being transformed.
Ideas and social conditions that have lasted for centuries
are quickly being replaced in our time
by new concepts of social organization.
City living is much more common today,
for example,
and even rural places have citylike lifestyles.
New and incredibly efficient media
make connections around the world possible
so that styles of thought and feeling
can be known worldwide
that were once limited in their scope.
Migration is increasing as well,
and this creates a socialization
that doesn't always include personal relationships.
And while what we describe here is true
in advanced nations,
it is rapidly becoming more and more true
worldwide.

7 So much change calls traditional values into question,
especially among young people
who are not satisfied to wait until adulthood
to take their role in this dynamic.
Hence, the handing down of teachings and traditions
is more difficult than ever before.
Religion is also affected, of course,
by this new world movement.
On one hand, superstitious and magical views of the world
are eradicated by science and knowledge,
which purify faith in the unseen God.
On the other hand, growing numbers of people
are abandoning religion

in favor of science or humanism.
Evidence of this disturbing trend
    is found in literature,
        art,
        the humanities,
        history,
        and even in civil law.

8 All these modern developments,
    coming so rapidly and disorderly,
    intensify imbalances within the human person.
One's intellect, for example, may be thoroughly modern,
    while one's theory of meaning is more traditional,
        and no joining of the two seems possible.
Or one's concern for practicality and efficiency
    is in tension with one's moral conscience.
Or the demands of collective existence
    conflict with one's need for personal thought,
        or even contemplation.
Furthermore, the family is in tension
    with pressures on it from many sides:
        population control,
        economic realities,
        or social demands.
Likewise, tensions emerge among nations
    when some are so wealthy and others so poor.
All of this leads to mistrust,
    division,
    and hardship,
        and humans are at once the cause
        and the victims of it all.

9 For the first time in history,
    many believe it is possible and desirable

that the benefits of modern culture
    can be extended to everyone.
And those who do not yet have these benefits want them,
    especially
        the world's starving people,
        women,
        workers,
        and farmers.
There is also a movement for a universal community
    in which persons can live a full and free life.
In all of this,
    the modern world is both powerful and weak,
    capable of noble deeds or foul ones,
    in the path of freedom or that of slavery.
Modern people seek new levels of meaning today
    precisely because of the unleashed powers
        of modern life,
        which can either serve us or destroy us.

10 The modern condition is rooted
    in the nature of human life itself:
    boundless in ambition yet limited,
    attracted to many things,
        but forced to choose among them,
        often choosing those things
            known to be harmful.
Many who choose practical materialism
    do not even give this matter thought!
Others are weighed down by unhappiness
    and do not have the emotional wherewithal
        to consider it.
Still others believe human effort alone
    is sufficient to order society
    and bring meaning and peace to humankind.

And some believe there is no meaning in life
    to begin with.
Yet there are those, increasing in number, who ask:
    "What is the human person?
    What is this sense of sorrow,
        of evil,
        of death,
            which continues to exist despite progress?
    What victory have we won in these times,
        and at what cost?
    What can we expect from life,
        what can we offer to it?
    What follows our earthly life?"

We in the Church firmly believe
    that the Light of Christ can illumine our search.
Beneath these many changes and developments
    is an unchanging and loving God,
    and we now speak of these matters
        in order to cooperate in finding the solution
        to the outstanding problems of our age.

Part One: The Church and Humankind's Vocation

11 We begin our inquiry with the People of God,
    which believes it is led by the Holy Spirit.
This People of God,
    this human family of which we are part,
    makes careful inquiry into the events,
        needs,
        and desires of this age
    to find authentic signs of God's presence here:
Who are we humans, anyway?

What does society need today to be better?
What do human actions throughout the world mean?
People are waiting for answers to these questions,
    and by this inquiry, it will become clear
    that the Church and the world
        render service to each other,
        for the mission of the Church is religious
        but is also supremely human!

Chapter One
THE DIGNITY OF THE HUMAN PERSON

12 Everyone on earth believes
    with nearly unanimous opinion
    that the human person is the center and crown
        of the earth.
But what is the human person?
There are divergent views among people about this,
    some exalting the human person
    as the measure of all things
        and others debasing human nature
        to the point of despair.
We take a positive view of the human person,
    based on the words of our Scriptures,
    expressed in the Book of Genesis,
    that God created us in the divine likeness
        and was pleased with the outcome.
We understand ourselves, furthermore,
    to be essentially social creatures,
    created from the beginning to have companions.

13 But there is more.

The human person quickly attempted to separate
   from the Creator
   and chose to oppose God,
      according to our scriptural stories.
Human experience agrees with this:
   for when we examine our hearts,
   we do indeed find an inclination toward
      disrupted relationships
      and darkness.
We find ourselves split within ourselves,
   caught in a dramatic struggle of good versus evil,
   light versus darkness.
And into this situation,
   we believe God sent Jesus Christ,
   the Light of the World,
      to strengthen us with grace
      and to free us from the darkness.

14 For the human person,
   although composed of both body and soul,
      is a unified, whole person,
      not divided.
We are obliged to love our bodies and, indeed,
   the whole material world,
   for it is created by God too.
Nevertheless, it is often there,
   in the material, physical realm,
   that we find inclinations toward darkness.
So we must probe our human nature to its depth
   to find our souls,
   and when we do, we will not be mocked,
      for there in the depth of our hearts,
      we also find God.

15 We can conclude from this plunging into our depths
    that in some ways
    we humans surpass the material universe
    and share in the light of the divine mind.
We have made great progress in many arenas,
    using our talents,
    and we continue to win enormous victories
        in science, technology, and the liberal arts.
Nonetheless, we continue to search
    for penetrating truths
        and find them!
We can look beyond observable data
    and employ the wisdom
    that perfects our intelligence,
        and it is this wisdom
        that we now need so badly
            or the world may perish.
Wise men and women must come forth
    to lead us in this age,
    and they may well come from less developed places
        where wisdom often thrives.
This wisdom leads us to desire goodness and truth.

16 In the depths of our conscience,
    we detect a law
    which we have not laid upon ourselves
    but which we must obey.
Its voice, ever calling us to love
    and to do what is good and avoid evil,
    is heard at the right moments in our lives.
It speaks to our hearts: "Do this; shun that."
For this law, written into our very hearts,
    is from God.
Our very dignity comes from observing this inner law,

and by it we will be judged.
Conscience is our most secret core and sanctuary.
It is where we are alone with God,
    whose voice echoes in our depths.
The voice we hear will always,
    in a variety of ways,
    call us to love God and neighbor well.
By being faithful to it,
    we are joined with all of humanity
    in a great human search
        for truth
        and for genuine solutions
            to the vexing problems
            of modern life.
It is clear from what we are saying here
    that we must be faithful, then,
    to that inner voice,
        that "divine guide" in our souls,
        and not allow our clarity to be dulled
        by repeated acts that are contrary to love.
We must not allow our souls
    to be nibbled away by acts of hate and selfishness.

17 The key to this is freedom.
Authentic human freedom does not mean
    "doing whatever we please."
Rather, it flows from attentive listening
    to our conscience,
    as well as in doing what our conscience directs.
Such free choices will always be fully human ones
    and will not result from impulsive actions
        or from external rules.
We humans have the potential to spontaneously
    choose Good

with God as our inner guide.

18 It is in the face of death
that all this is brought into sharp relief and focus,
for death eventually claims us all
and none of our technology can stop it.
And even if we could prolong life,
we would still be possessed of an innate sense
of a higher life in the divine love.
For we believe that God created us for eternal life,
where the wholeness we lose through sin
will be restored
because of the mercy of Christ.
Faith, therefore, fills thoughtful people with hope
and unites them with all who have already died.

19 For our lives flow from the creative energy
of this faith
and return there as well
in an intimate and eternal linkage.
Because we believe this link with God
is vital for human happiness and fulfillment,
we want to examine atheism in all its forms.
We consider it one of the most serious problems
of this age.
There are many kinds of atheism,
some very subtle forms and others more blatant.
There are those, for example,
who expressly deny the existence of God at all
but others who simply argue
that we can know nothing at all about God,
whoever God may be.
Others believe that all truths can be explained by reason
or even that there is no absolute truth to explain

in the first place!
Some hold humanity in such high regard
    that they have left only an anemic faith in God,
    though they may not deny God outrightly.
And still others simply have no religious stirrings,
    no desire to ask these questions at all.

20 Modern atheism confuses human freedom
    with our relationship to God
    as though the two cannot coexist.
It claims that men and women will be freed
    by economic gains
    or social advancement.

21 But we believe and have always taught
    that the true nature of humans
    is to be joined with the divine life force,
        that real freedom comes in this.
We continue to teach this,
    and we assert firmly that any other approach
    robs human persons of their dignity
    and offers them only economic or social solutions
        to situations demanding more!
22 We believe that hoping in eternal life
    does not diminish human life here and now
    but propels us to live with great nobility
        because when we die we take with us
        the love we have in our hearts.
Without this hope, indeed,
    the riddles of life and death,
    of guilt and of grief,
        go unresolved
        and people often succumb to despair.
Our lives remain unsolved puzzles,

especially when major life events unfold for us.
We come to understand ourselves
more and more
only with the wisdom of God.
So the remedy that we apply to atheism is twofold:
the proper presentation of the Church's teaching
and well-lived Christian lives.
People will see us believers,
as they did the martyrs and others in the past;
they will see our unity and charity,
and come to believe themselves.

For us Christians,
the truth and meaning of our lives
is wrapped up in the mystery of Christ,
the Incarnate Word of God.
In Christ, the riddles of sorrow and death
take on meaning,
the divine presence is made profoundly clear,
and we find the energy and power to live fully.
In Christ, we become capable of being fully human,
sharing in the full divinity,
divinity made flesh,
working with human hands,
thinking with a human mind,
acting by human choice,
and, above all, loving with a human heart.
What greater love do we need?
What greater truth?
The mystery of the human person
is centered in this divine core,
revealed through Christ,
and stirring us to full humanity.

Chapter Two
THE COMMUNITY OF HUMANKIND

23–24 There is a growing interdependence
among people today
which is based on the many technological advances
that are obvious to everyone.
But this interdependence reaches its perfection
only in growing human relationships,
not merely scientific ones.
For God, we believe, desires that all people
become one family
with love for God and neighbor as the basis.
We cannot separate these two:
whoever loves God must love neighbor
or the love is false.
Jesus said as much himself.
It is obvious how important this is
as we come to rely more on each other
and grow in unity.
Because of Jesus' prayer
"that all may be one as we are one,"
new horizons are now opened for us,
implying that we will reach our true destiny
only by pursuing such oneness
with each other.
25 So we humans, in order to fully discover ourselves,
must donate ourselves to one another in love.
This aspect of human nature,
the social aspect,
suggests strongly that the advance of society
depends on individual persons progressing first.
After all, the whole purpose of social organizations
is to make human life more noble.

This social nature of which we speak
        makes it clear that the progress of the human person
        and the advance of society
            go hand in hand.
After all, the whole purpose of social institutions
        such as the family,
            political parties,
            labor organizations,
            and even the churches,
        is to enhance our lives
        as human persons.
Indeed, some of these social institutions
        arise from the very intrinsic nature of being human.
            The family is one of these,
            as is the political community.
Other social institutions are created by us
        to serve our needs,
        and our participation in them is more voluntary.
And both of these are on the rise today,
        increasing both in number and influence.
Even though this is true, however,
        it is also true today
        that men and women are often diverted
            from doing good
            and spurred toward doing evil,
            and the cause of this is the very social order
                in which they live
                and into which they have been born.
There are natural tensions in any social plan,
        especially economic life,
            political organization,
            and various social groups.
These are the tensions that often yield
        to a breakdown in human nature,

based on human pride and selfishness
   which contaminate these social activities.
      Sin results.
Sin can be overcome
   only by steady effort with the help of grace.
26 There is a condition in human life that we call
   the common good.
By this term, we refer to that set of conditions
   of human life,
   economic, social, political, and others,
   which, taken together,
      makes it possible for us
      to become all we are created to be,
         to reach our human fulfillment.
Various social groups
   approach the common good differently
   and must take each other into account, therefore,
      if all humanity is to achieve it.
We recognize with increasing awareness today
   that there is a fundamental human dignity
   which must be in place for the common good
   to be possible in the first place.
This fundamental human dignity is universal
   and unchanging,
   based as it is in our created nature.
It leads us to say that everyone must have
   food, clothing, and shelter;
   the right to choose a state of life freely;
   the right to found a family;
   the right to education, employment,
      a good reputation, respect,
      and appropriate information;
   the right to follow one's own conscience;
   the right to the protection of privacy

and to rightful freedom,
        even in matters of religion.
Our point is becoming more clear here:
    all social organizing must be for the benefit
    of the human person,
    and it requires constant improvement.
It must be founded on truth,
    built on justice,
    animated by love,
    and growing in freedom.
And we realize that in order for this to be true today,
    substantial adjustments in attitude
    and abundant changes in current society
        will have to take place.
But we believe that God's Spirit
    continues to hover over this growth in human order
    and to renew the face of the earth.
And, furthermore, we believe that it is rooted
    in the very heart of men and women
    to seek increasing dignity,
        and not to sink into darkness.

27 In practical terms, this means
    that everyone must consider his or her neighbor,
        without exception,
        "another self."
Each person must take into account first of all
    the life of each other person
    and the means necessary to live with dignity.

It must not be with us as it was with the nameless rich man
    who saw Lazarus bleeding and hungry,
    without this dignity of which we speak here,
        and ignored him.

Remember what happened?
>
> Lazarus rested in the bosom of Abraham and Sarah
> while that rich man lived on in isolation,
>> selfishness,
>> and ignorance:
>>> hell.

In our times, this means we have a special obligation
> to make ourselves the neighbor of every person
>> without exception
> and to actively assist them when we meet them
>> in the path of our lives.

This includes old people abandoned by all,
> foreigners in our midst,
> refugees,
> children without parents,
> and hungry people.

All of these, when we see them and hear their cry,
> disturb our conscience
> and remind us of Jesus' teaching in Matthew 25:
>> "As long as you did it for one of these,
>>> . . . you did it for me."

And not only that.

We must also work to defeat
> any force opposed to life itself,
> such as any kind of murder,
>> genocide,
>> abortion,
>> euthanasia,
>> or willful self-destruction.

We must work to defeat
> whatever violates human dignity,
> such as mutilation,
>> mental or physical torture,
>> coercion of the will,

subhuman living conditions,
arbitrary imprisonment,
deportation,
slavery,
prostitution,
the selling of women and children,
and disgraceful working conditions.
All of these poison human society,
doing harm to both those afflicted by them
and those perpetrating them.
They are, in short, a supreme dishonor
to the Creator God.

28 We should also have respect and love
for those who think differently than we do
in social,
political,
or even religious matters.
In fact, the more deeply we understand others,
the more we can dialogue with them,
seeking understanding.
This is not to say we should accept
untruth as truth
or meanness as goodness.
But the people whom we believe to be in untruth
are dignified nonetheless,
and we teach that only God can make judgment
in the end.
God alone is the searcher of the human heart,
and we should not make judgments
about the internal guilt of anyone.
To the contrary,
we are taught by Jesus to love
even those we consider our enemies.

29 Every person has a soul and is created in God's image.
    All people are of the same nature and origin.
Having been offered a unique relationship
    of sonship and daughtership with God by Christ,
    all likewise have the same divine calling.
There is, therefore, a basic equality of all human persons
    regardless of social or cultural background,
        race,
        gender,
        color,
        language,
        or religion.
All discrimination should be overcome
    and eradicated,
    and we regret that so many human rights
        are not being honored around the world,
        especially for women who are not free
            to choose a husband freely,
            to embrace a state of life,
            to acquire an education,
            or to enjoy cultural benefits
                equal to men.
As we have made clear above,
    human institutions, both private and public,
    must labor to enhance the dignity and purpose
    of all women and men.

30 A purely private sense of morality cannot exist
    in this day and age
    because of the interdependence we have
        on one another.
Each of us must not only fulfill our human call
    to live justly and with love
    but must also work to insure that social institutions

are more fair.
Each of us contributes to the common good
    when we use our abilities
    in this way.
We should pay our just share of taxes,
    obey social laws,
    and conduct our business honestly.
We should operate our industry with an eye to
    the protection of human health around us.
It even comes down to obeying speed limits
    so that those around us are not in danger.
31 In sum, we call on everyone to consider it
    his or her sacred obligation
    to esteem and observe social needs.
If all do, a truly new and more humane society
    will be available to all.
For this to happen,
    education must be widespread,
    especially for youth of every background.
Likewise, neither destitution nor sumptuousness
    is our aim
    but the building up of the common good.
Hence, the desire to take part in organizing society
    should be encouraged for everyone,
    and we offer special praise for those nations
        that allow the fullest possible participation
        in governance and public affairs.
32 Once again we point out that God did not create humans
    to live in isolation
    but in community.
We are not individuals set side by side
    without bonds or links,
    but rather, we are bound together
        as a single people,

with one common inner principle, the Spirit.
This communal nature of ours
  finds its fullest expression in Jesus Christ,
  who lived in radical human fellowship.
The lifestyle, friendships, and social engagements of Jesus
  point the way for us:
  we are to live as one Body,
      members of one another,
        rendering mutual service to each other
            based on our gifts.
And this communal solidarity in Christ
  must be increased steadily
  until we live fully with God as one family.

Chapter Three
HUMAN ACTIVITY THROUGHOUT THE WORLD

33 Men and women have ceaselessly labored
  to improve their lives,
  using their talents and hard work to do so.
Today that work is paying off more than ever,
  and nearly every aspect of human life
  has come under our control
      through science and technology.
Little by little the worldwide human family
  is realizing that it is indeed just that,
  a family united by common concerns.
The result of this is that many phenomena
  which were once attributed to divine power
  are now fully understood to be of human making.
But all of this leaves us with certain nagging questions
  about life, meaning, and the end goal of it all.

The Church stands in the midst of these questions
    and offers guidance,
    without having all the solutions.
The Church can offer principles for proceeding
    and wants to add to the human journey
    the light of truth
        so that we do not wander in darkness.
34 Christians are convinced that the triumphs
    of human endeavor,
    the wonderful advances of society,
    and the monumental efforts
        to produce a better world
        are completely in accord with God's will.
It is the very mission of the human person
    to understand and use the benefits of creation
        to the good of all.
Therefore, in everyday life,
    as well as in more dramatic ways,
    when we work for our livelihoods,
    God is present, unfolding ongoing creative work.
Hence, far from thinking that such human advances
    are in opposition to God's desires,
    we are convinced they are a sign of God's grace.
We therefore say with confidence
    that we are not hindered from improving the world
        by the Christian message
        but, on the contrary, bound to do just that.

35 Human activity, to be sure,
    flows from people and benefits people.
When someone works,
    he or she alters things and society,
    but he or she also develops his or her very self.
In a word, she or he grows,

and this growth is more valuable
than the external wealth it produces.
A person is more precious for what she or he is
than for what he or she has.
Likewise, then, we also believe
that whatever is done to obtain justice,
to establish a broader solidarity,
and to make living conditions more humane
is more valuable than technology.
We can, therefore, draw this principle from our thinking:
all human endeavor is of God
when it allows men and women
to pursue their created purpose
and follow it to fulfillment.

36 Many modern people seem to fear
that a closer bond between human activity
and religion
will work against independence in science.
We have sometimes even been led by certain Christians
to believe that faith and science oppose one another
but we do not agree with this at all.
The deep realities of society and science
are deciphered by us little by little,
and this gradual discovery of the universe
is our natural instinct
and also, we believe, God's will.
Whoever works to learn about the world in this way,
even if they are unaware of it,
is nevertheless being led by the hand of God
in whom everything continues in being
and finds its ultimate meaning.
If such methodological study is carried out
in a genuinely scientific way

and follows moral norms,
then it is of God.
But if the scientist denies the place of the divine
in his or her work,
it is false,
because apart from the Creator,
creation no longer exists.
When God is forgotten, human life loses meaning.

37 We know from our Scriptures and our history
that we humans seem bound to wrestle constantly
with selfish desires.
When these self-centered ways of behaving emerge in us,
they threaten the peace and security of our race,
and this is especially true today.
Hence, the world has not yet become a place
of true sisterhood and brotherhood.
So we must wrestle with dark desires
made manifest in a spirit of vanity and malice,
and it at this very point that the Church
offers us a helping hand.
In order to overcome this tendency toward darkness,
we must come to Christ.
By this we mean that our motives and actions
are made more pure and perfect
when we realize that everything we have
comes from God
and is intended for us to share.
Such an attitude makes us free and humble:
free to receive everything
and humble to know its source is not ourselves.

38 For Christ has shown us the way of love,
and the law of love is the basic law

of human growth, development, and transformation.
To those who believe in divine love,
    Christ has shown that the hope of a world
    based on love
        is not a foolish hope.
This hope must be pursued in common, everyday life
    as we "lay down our lives" for one another,
    having learned to do this from Christ
        and believing that doing so
        will lead all to a glorious shared life.
Christ is present in the midst of this,
    providing the energy we need,
    arousing the desire for good in us,
    animating our hearts,
    and purifying our noble longings
        for human solidarity.
This work is done by Christ in the hearts of people
    by the power of the Holy Spirit.
This Spirit first arouses in us
    the desire for a better world
    but also encourages the best and most noble
        of our sentiments
        so they will be used toward this end:
            to make Christ present.
And this divine presence of Christ
    is nowhere more profound
    than in the Eucharist itself,
        where indeed the natural elements
        of bread and wine
        are changed into a meal of solidarity!

39 All of this is so important to us
    because of our belief
    that the world in which we now live

is but a foreshadowing of what is to come.
We believe that the betterment of this world
 is God's will and desire,
  for it makes us humans more noble
   and prepares us for an eternity
   on this same path of wholeness
   and holiness.

Chapter Four
THE ROLE OF THE CHURCH
IN THE MODERN WORLD

40 Everything we have said about the human person,
 about human dignity,
 human community,
 and the meaning of human activity
  now serves as the foundation
  for what we wish to say here.
We will speak about the place of the Church in the world
 and the dialogue between them.
As we make our comments now,
 we also base them on what we have said
 about the nature of the Church
  as a sign to the world
  of the presence of God.
The Church, as we have already said,
 emerges from God's love for us
 and God's desire that we form a divine family
  during our lifetimes.
The Church is thus a leaven and a soul
 for human society
 and, as such, that part of the Church

which is found on earth, here and now,
and that part which is to come
in heaven later,
penetrate each other.
This is most evident in the Church's task
of elevating and healing the dignity of being human
and insisting on this point,
even in the face of darkness.
The Church offers deep meaning and purpose
to those who hear her word
and contributes greatly to making the human family
more human!
This is a two-way relationship:
the Church assists the world,
and the world assists the Church
interdependently.
And this applies to the Roman Catholic Church
but also to other church bodies
who have the same goal.
41 We now intend to set forth certain principles
for the proper fostering of this mutual exchange
between the churches and the world.

Members of the human family today
are on the road to a more thorough development
of their personalities
and to a growing discovery and absolute claim
on basic human rights.
These ultimate goals of being human
are written on the heart;
they are part and parcel of life,
the fundamental meaning of existence,
and the innermost nature of humankind.
We believe that only God can lead us

to this truth;
only God provides an answer to the riddle of life.
The Church is a stable force
that steadfastly maintains human dignity
even in the face of fluctuating trends in society
regarding the value of life
and the human body.
No one can protect humans from exploitation
better than those who speak for God,
and today that is the Gospel of Christ,
entrusted to the Church.
The Gospel has a sacred reverence
for the dignity of conscience
and its freedom of choice.
It announces and proclaims the freedom
of the sons and daughters of God,
and it rejects wholeheartedly all forms of slavery,
internal and external,
which result from human mistakes.
By virtue of this Gospel,
the Church proclaims the rights of humankind.
It acknowledges and affirms those movements today
that support and foster these rights,
desiring to penetrate them
with the spirit of the Gospel
so that we do not wander into the belief
that our rights are ensured
only when we are also free of divine law.
Indeed, divine law is most natural to humans
and without it the dignity of the human person
will perish.

42 The Church is not tied to any specific system
of government,

economics,
or social order.
The purpose that Christ gave the Church
is, indeed, only a religious one.
But out of that mission
can come a light and clarity to guide others
and the energy of love to serve as their center.
As a matter of fact, the Church can and should
undertake certain works herself,
such as assisting the poor and suffering.
We see an evolution in the world today
toward unity
which pleases us because the innermost nature
of the Church
is the promotion of unity.
And since the Church is committed to no single system
of governance,
she can bridge them all,
serving as catalyst.
We therefore urge all women and men
to put strife and division aside
and live together in peace.
This council looks with great respect on all that is true,
good,
and just in social systems everywhere.
The Church is willing to promote and assist these systems
and has no fiercer desire than to develop freely
under every system that grants recognition
to the basic rights of person and family
and the demands of the common good.

43 We Christians believe that these times and this life
will ultimately end in an eternal dwelling place.
Nonetheless, we also believe that life in this world

and in these times
must be lived nobly, fully,
and with attention to our day-to-day obligations.
And we also believe that religion and everyday life
are intimately and indissolubly linked,
part and parcel of each other.
We cannot divorce what happens in religion
from how we live our everyday life.
Simply put, there is no split between faith
and everyday life.
Jesus himself repeatedly warned against
dividing life and religious belief in this way.
So did the prophets of the time before Christ!
Therefore, let there be no false distinctions
between one's professional and social life
and one's religious life.
If you neglect your temporal duties,
you also neglect your spiritual ones!
It behooves us Christians, then,
to become skilled at our trades,
to pay attention to developing expertise,
and to use it wisely.
Laypeople ought to follow their well-formed consciences
so that the divine law
is lived out in everyday life,
looking to priests for spiritual nourishment,
but not imagining they have all the answers!
And when faithful people disagree,
and that will certainly be the case,
do not presume to speak for God or the Church
but try to enlighten one another
through honest discussion and charity,
always earnest in your search for truth.
In this way, laypeople, guided by their pastors

who are guided by their bishops,
will indeed animate the world
with a Christian spirit.
Pastors and bishops, therefore,
must remember that their daily conduct
reflects the Gospel and greatly influences others.
We believe the Church has always been
a faithful lover of Jesus
and an everlasting sign of salvation.
But we are also aware that some of her pastors,
as well as laypeople,
have not always been faithful to this love;
some have failed to live out the very message
that they are bound to preach!
However history judges them,
we should be aware of this
and work to improve such failings,
purifying and renewing ourselves
so that the Light of Christ
can indeed shine through us all!

44 As we have just described it,
the Church can add greatly to the modern world,
but the modern world can also benefit
the Church.
The progress of science
and the treasures hidden in various forms
of human culture
reveal new roads to truth.
The Church wants to speak in the language of the people
and needs the help
of those versed in varying specialties
to do this.
Because change occurs so rapidly today

and thought patterns differ so widely,
the Church needs to increase the activity
of adapting herself to this age.
To do this, she calls for help
from the people living in the world
who understand these times so well.
In this way, the Church is enriched
by the development of human social life,
and all those who promote the values of the Gospels,
however that is done,
benefit the mission of the Church as well.
The Church has a visible social structure
which is a sign of its unity in Christ.
Because of this social nature,
we know that whoever contributes
to the development of humankind on the level of
family,
culture,
economic and social life,
or national or international politics,
when they order these
according to the plan of God,
also contributes to the life of the Church herself.
Even those who persecute the Church
in some ways assist her.

45 In all this,
the Church's assistance to the world
and the world's assistance to the Church,
there is one single intention on our part:
that God's Reign be established
and that all men and women
be made whole.
For the end of everything is life in God;

for us this means life in Christ.
Christ is the answer to our longings,
   the center of the human race,
   the joy of every heart.
Enlivened and joined in Christ's Spirit,
   we recognize that, indeed,
   Christ is the Alpha and the Omega,
   the beginning and the end of all that is.

Part Two: Some Problems of Special Urgency

Preface

46 Having spoken in the council
   about the dignity of the human person
   and the work that all people are called to do
      both as individuals and members of society,
      we now turn our attention
      to five specific questions:
         marriage and the family;
         human culture;
         social, political, and economic life;
         bonds among the nations;
         war and peace.
We hope to speak of these under the Light of Christ
   so that Christians may be properly guided
   and all humankind enlightened
      as we search for answers
      to complex questions.

Chapter One
FOSTERING THE NOBILITY OF MARRIAGE
AND THE FAMILY

47 Marriage and family life
    are the bedrock of a healthy human society,
    and we are pleased to see ways
        in which these "partnerships of love"
        are fostered today.
But there are also ways in which they are hindered,
    such as polygamy,
        divorce,
        so-called free love,
        excessive self-love,
        the idealizing of pleasure,
        and the illicit use of birth control.
It is also disrupted by
    modern economic conditions,
    social and psychological influences,
    the demands of civil society,
    and problems resulting from population growth.
In each of these cases,
    an anguish of conscience results for many
    which is terribly painful and disruptive.
By reflecting on key points
    (though not on all related matters),
    we wish to support marriage and family life.

48 The partnership of married life and love,
    first of all,
    is created by God
    and rooted in sexual union
        when there is permanent,
            personal,
            and mutual consent.

Once agreed to, this bond is no longer purely human
 but now takes on a divine nature
 and is oriented toward having children
  and forming a family.
The two married partners render mutual service
 to each other
 through their sexual love and daily life,
  leading them to total fidelity
  and unbreakable oneness.
Love of this sort wells up
 from the fountain of divine love
 that flows from Christ
  so that authentic married love
  comes from God.
It is for this reason that the Church
 treats marriage as a sacrament,
 a sign of God's faithful love of us,
 and a source of grace for the partners.
The love present in marriage is, then,
 really divine love
 expressed through sex and mutuality
 and lived out in the raising of the family.
Children, likewise, contribute in their own way
 to making their parents and the entire family holy.
Families thus share an interdependence,
 providing support in hard times
 and sharing everyday life.

49 The love that a married couple shares
 is expressed and made perfect
 through sexual intercourse,
  of which the Scriptures speak glowingly
  and which unites human and divine
   in mutual giving and bliss.

This is not mere eroticism,
    which ultimately fades,
    but involves the whole person
    in faithfulness and richness
        otherwise not known to humans.
Supported by mutual fidelity
    and made holy through the sacrament of matrimony,
    this love continues as the couple is faithful
        in both mind and body,
        in good times and in bad.
It therefore excludes either adultery or divorce.
Children should be taught about this
    so they, too, can enter marriages that are holy.
50 Marriage has several ends,
    none of more or less account than the others.
Very important among them is the task of transmitting life
    and educating those
    to whom it has been transmitted.
In this, parents cooperate in creation,
    a divine activity,
    and must enter into this thoughtfully.
They should take into account those already born
    and those foreseen,
        considering both the material and spiritual conditions
        of the times
        and of their family's state.
They then consult the interests of the family group,
    of temporal society,
    and of the Church's teachings.
The parents should, then, ultimately make this judgment
    in the sight of God,
        following their conscience,
            enlightened by divine law,
            and guided by the Church.

Thus, parents sometimes stop having children
    and yet maintain their love,
      for the purpose of marriage is not solely tied
        to procreation.
The mutual love of the spouses, too,
    must be embodied in a right manner;
    it must grow and ripen.

[51] This can be very difficult if sexual loving is ended
    in order to prevent conception
    and can endanger the bond
      as well as the quality of family life.
We reject wholeheartedly a solution to this
    that involves the taking of life
    through abortion or the killing of infants.
Since the transmission of human life
    is not merely a human activity,
    sexual intercourse and responsible conception
      must be harmonized.
Decisions made toward this end
    will be based on objective standards
      that reflect divine love.
Catholics are not allowed to use methods of birth regulation
    that are disapproved of
    by the teaching authority of the Church.
How all of this will be understood in our day and age
    has been handed over to a special commission
    which will report soon to the pope,
      and for that reason,
      this is all we will say here about it.

[52] The family is a school of deeper humanity
    and needs the communion of minds
    and joint decisions of spouses

as well as the cooperation of the children
  to be maintained.
Having the father present is essential,
  and allowing the mother her domestic role
  is also needed,
    though this should not undermine
    the legitimate social progress of women.
Children should be prepared for independence
  and not forced into marriage.
Hence families are the foundation of society,
  and governments should support them.
Those skilled in science, too,
  can support the regulation of births
  and peace of conscience,
    especially those in medicine,
    biology,
    social science,
    and psychology.
Organizations outside the family can also offer support,
  especially for children and spouses.
And, finally, spouses themselves,
  joined in authentic sexual love,
  harmony of mind,
  and mutual holiness,
    witness to the presence of God
    and the mystery of love.

Chapter Two
THE PROPER DEVELOPMENT OF CULTURE

53 The cultivation of the goods and values of nature
  are the basis of the authentic human person.

People live in both culture and nature.
There are, of course, numerous cultures,
    each having a historical aspect
        as well as a social dimension,
        a sociological sense,
        and a unique ethnic character.
All culture implies "community living"
    and includes patterns for sharing wealth,
    various ways of laboring,
        of language,
        of religious practice,
        of forming customs,
        of making laws and courts,
        of advancing the arts, sciences, and beauty.
54 Because of all the changes that have taken place recently
    in social and cultural life,
    we can actually call this a "new age"
    in human history.
The enormous growth of natural, human, and social science
    not to mention communications and technology,
        has paved the way
        for a modern refinement of culture.
Critical judgment has been shaped to a fine edge
    by the exact sciences, for example.
Human behavior is explained more fully
    by psychological research.
Historical studies throw new light on our past,
    helping us see how changeable
        and evolutionary the world is.
All over the world, customs are more uniform,
    lifestyles are similarly urban,
    and new ways of thinking and using leisure
        are everywhere.
Thus, little by little, a more universal form

of human culture is developing
through which the unity of humankind
is being fostered.
55 We are increasingly aware
that we are the authors of this new culture,
that we are directly responsible for it
and will live under it.
There is a new humanism in the world today
which defines us first and foremost
as responsible for each other.

56 All of this raises some difficult new questions
for us today.
How can we continue to increase exchange among cultures
while at the same time
maintain the identity of the small community,
preserve ancestral wisdom,
and save the uniqueness of each people?
How can the vitality and growth of a new culture
harmonize with the heritage of tradition?
How can branches of knowledge shoot out so quickly
while at the same time we undertake
a necessary synthesis of them
so men and women can still grow in wisdom
through contemplation and wonder?
How can all women and men on earth share somehow
in the new technology?
And finally, how will we maintain the independence
that culture claims for itself
without developing a humanism devoid of God?

57 Here are some principles that we can follow
to begin to offer answers to these questions.

First of all,
    faith and culture work together
    with many of the same aims and goals.
The fact that faith points people toward divine life
    does not diminish people's attention to human life,
        because the two are intimately linked.
Most aspects of culture elevate the human family
    to a more sublime understanding
        of truth, goodness, beauty, and fairness.
Even though there is a temptation in science
    and under modern scientific thinking
    to doubt everything not observable,
        nonetheless it also prepares us
        to remain close to God.
Furthermore, modern advancements
    provide many positive values,
    including the study of science,
        fidelity to truth in this study,
        teamwork in technology,
        international solidarity,
        the role of experts in helping all,
        and an eagerness to improve
            the human standard of living.

58 Second, the Church is not bound
    to any particular culture or period of history;
    human culture and religious culture advance
        as one reality.
The Good News of Christ
    mixes with life and human culture
    to combat and remove error and evil,
    to purify and elevate the morality of peoples,
    and to assist spiritual qualities to blossom.

59 Third, the purpose of culture
    is the benefit of humans,
    the good of the community and of society.
It is the role of culture to develop
    the human spirit of wonder,
        understanding,
        contemplation,
        the formation of personal judgments,
        and the development of a religious,
            moral,
            and social sense of self.
Toward this end,
    the rights of the individual
    and the needs of the community
        are both safeguarded
        within the limits of the common good.
Cultural development requires that a certain freedom
    be in place,
    freedom to search for truth,
        voice one's mind,
        and publicize one's beliefs.
Public authority should make this possible everywhere.

60 Because it is possible today
    to liberate most people from ignorance,
    Christians have the urgent duty to provide education
        wherever it is needed.
This will make it possible for a fuller participation
    in cultural life for many people
        who otherwise would not be included,
        especially country people and laborers,
            as well as women.
Regarding women especially,
    everyone is responsible to ensure

that their specific role in cultural life
    is fostered.

61 With so much new knowledge today,
    almost no one can grasp it all
    and unify all aspects of human understanding
        in his or her thinking.
Nonetheless, it is essential that we maintain a view
    of humans as whole persons,
    including intellect, will, and conscience.
Taking advantage of increased leisure
    for reading,
    sports, and physical activities,
    time with family,
    and travel
        will enrich people and help them reach
        an emotional balance.

62 It has proven difficult sometimes
    to harmonize culture with the Church,
    but it is necessary to do that.
Recent studies and findings of science,
    history,
    and philosophy
        raise new questions about life
        and demand new theological investigations.
Furthermore, theologians are invited
    to find more suitable ways
    to communicate doctrine to the people
        of their times.
The Deposit of Faith or revealed truths are one thing
    but the manner in which they are expressed
        is another.
Pastors can employ psychology and sociology

to more effectively bring faith to life.
Literature and the arts can elevate men and women
    to new planes of understanding
    about our place in history
        and the meaning of these times.
The Church should give recognition, therefore,
    to these arts, including new artistic forms,
    and introduce them into the sanctuary
        when appropriate.
Christ's faithful can thereby live in closer union
    with their neighbors
    if religious practice and morality keep pace
        with science and its theories.
Theological inquiry should seek a profound understanding
    of revealed truth
    without neglecting close contact with its own times.
Laypeople ought to be trained in the sacred sciences
    and some will deepen these studies
    by their own labors.
And, finally, everyone possesses
    a lawful freedom of inquiry and thought
    and the freedom to express their minds humbly
        but with courage
        about those matters
            in which they enjoy competence.

Chapter Three
SOCIO-ECONOMIC LIFE

63 Once again in the arena of economics,
    we declare that the dignity and wholeness
    of the human person

must be honored as the center of focus.
As we have noted in other areas of human activity,
the economic life of women and men
is characterized by
an increasing domination of nature,
closer and more intense ties among citizens,
more mutual interdependence among nations,
and frequent government intervention.
At the same time, there has been great economic progress
which has made it possible to provide
for the increasing needs of the human race.
Still, there are reasons for anxiety today.
Many people are so captivated by their economic lives
that they seem nearly hypnotized by it,
both in wealthy nations as well as poorer ones.
We have the ability to make everyone on earth
economically comfortable,
yet so often a minority is served
and a majority suffer.
Hence, luxury and misery rub shoulders,
and while the wealthy are able to choose
among competing economic goods,
the deprived have almost no such choices
and live in subhuman conditions.
There often seems to be a lack of balance even within a nation
among various industries:
farming,
manufacturing,
and service industries.
And the imbalance among nations
threatens the peace of the world!
Because all of this is true,
this council now turns its attention
to this important and dynamic human activity

to reinforce certain principles
    and set forth certain guidelines
        to assist in economic development.

64 First and foremost,
    technical progress must be fostered
    to make it more possible to provide for all.
Along with this, a spirit of initiative,
    an eagerness to create and expand enterprises,
    the adaptation of methods of production,
    and the hard work of all who engage in production,
        all of these must be fostered too.
But here is the principle:
    the purpose of this is not to make anyone rich;
    it is not to give some the means of dominating others.
The purpose of this is to be in the service of all humans
    in terms of their intellectual,
        moral,
        and religious lives.
Economic development must, therefore,
    be carried out according to clear moral standards
    so that God's desire for humans is realized.

65 Not only that, but second,
    economic development must be under the control
    of the human family, working together,
        not left to the sole judgment of a few
        who possess economic or political power.
Within a nation, the citizens must decide these matters
    together among themselves.
Among nations, all affected parties should participate.
In all cases, people and their rights come first
    and production is the secondary aim.
Citizens have the right and duty to contribute

to economic development and production
according to their skills. .
Those with the means to do so
should not let their investment funds lay fallow
but should put them to use to employ others!

66 Third, and very importantly,
vigorous efforts must be made as quickly as possible
to reduce or remove
the immense economic inequalities
that now exist.
The demands of justice require this.
In particular, farmers and country people
must be helped to receive their just compensation.
Immigrant or migrant workers should be welcomed
and discrimination against them avoided,
and they should not be treated as mere tools
of production.
And in all places,
leaders should take care to provide suitable work
for all who are capable of it.
In situations where industry is changing quickly,
as in the use of automation, for example,
care should be taken that workers still have labor.
And those who are unable to work,
who are old or infirm,
should also be cared for.

67 Fourth, it is our clear principle
that human labor as a part of production
is superior to other elements
of economic life.
It is ordinarily by her or his labors
that a woman or man supports herself or himself.

It is also how humans serve one another,
    join together in common efforts of charity,
    and become partners in God's unfolding creation.
Jesus himself was such a worker.
Hence, everyone has a duty to work,
    and society has a duty to make work available
    and to be certain that wages are fair.
Toward this end and in keeping with principles of justice,
    working conditions must be suitable and safe,
    and economic slavery must be ended.
In fact, the work life should be adapted
    to the needs of the persons doing it,
    especially mothers and the aged.
Finally, workers should be able to develop as persons
    through their labors
    and to have ample leisure time
        for family, cultural life, and prayer.

68 Fifth, workers themselves should share
        in the decision making that affects their workplace
        as well as their industry.
Freely founded labor unions are a human right
    and provide an orderly way
    for workers to participate
    as long as their means is peaceful
        and conflict is resolved through negotiation
        and without resort to violence.
Workers have the right to elect their own representatives
    to these unions
    and to be part of them without reprisal.

69 Sixth, the earth and all it contains
    are meant for all to share fairly.
Whatever forms of ownership are followed,

attention must always be paid
to this universal purpose,
and all the goods of the earth
should benefit all the people of the earth.
Hence, we are bound to come to the relief of the poor
and to do so not only out of our leftovers
but out of our very subsistence.
Today, the poor number among the majority
so that we call on all people and nations
with the means to do so
to undertake a genuine sharing
of their goods.
In less advanced societies,
customs that no longer work
should be updated so all are cared for.
Social services that support the family
should be encouraged everywhere
but not so much that the citizens
form negative attitudes toward society.

70 Seventh, toward this end,
the distribution of goods and services
around the world should not be limited to charity
but should be directed toward helping
people find employment
and sufficient income.
This will require economic planning
so that today's needs are not met
at the expense of tomorrow's.
Furthermore, underdeveloped nations
should receive special attention
in economic planning.
Special care should be taken that such nations
not suffer when money values decline.

71 Eighth, it is important for people to own the resources
     of their nations
     and to have some control over material goods.
Such private ownership
     or another form of private dominion
          over material goods
          provides a necessary independence.
It adds incentives for carrying on one's work
     and constitutes a prerequisite for civil liberties.
This is not to be seen to be in conflict
     with necessary public ownership
     of certain resources
          that serve the public good.
In situations where the majority own most of the land
     while the minority have none or very little,
     steps should be taken toward balance.
Often in these situations, the workers
     are paid too little to live on
     and lack decent housing
          while the owners and merchants
          take all the profits.
Some people live in virtual slavery as a result of this,
     and all gains in culture and dignity are impossible.
Reforms are to be instituted in these cases
     and may include the redivision of land,
     cooperative enterprises,
     or educational assistance to people
          to help make them more productive.

72 In closing this discussion of economic life,
     let us say that Christians who work for justice
     and take an active role in economic development
     are making a great contribution
          to the peace of the world

and the prosperity of humankind.
They help permeate the world
    with the spirit of the beatitudes
    and grow in love as they work for justice.

Chapter Four
THE LIFE OF THE POLITICAL COMMUNITY

73 Changes are taking place today
    in how people are governed,
    and these include a growing awareness
        of the rights of minorities
        and of people's desire for freedom,
        freedom of assembly,
            of common action,
            and of religion.
There seems to be a broader spirit of cooperation
    taking hold around the world
    based on people's inner sense of justice,
        goodness,
        and the common good.
The best way to achieve a political life
    that serves people
    is to foster an inner sense of justice,
        generosity,
        and service of others.
We also want to strengthen basic beliefs
    about the nature of politics
    and about the proper limits of governments.

74 Acting alone, individuals or families
    are not sufficiently able to establish

all that is needed for a fully human life.
Hence, we group together
  to provide for those conditions
  in which people can become their fully human,
    created,
      graced selves.
Authority in this common enterprise
  is a good thing and very much needed
  to prevent people from fighting
    as they pursue their own needs.
Such authority should function more as a moral force
  than as a tyrant.
Hence, the political community exists for the sake
  of the common good,
  not for its own sake,
  and when it is legally established in a nation,
    citizens are bound to obey it.
If such political authority exceeds it bounds
  and violates the rights or dignity of anyone,
  then citizens are bound to defend themselves
    against such abuses.
Whatever form of government is chosen in a nation,
  it should make people more civilized,
    peace-loving,
    and full of desire for the common good.
75 Political systems should act without discrimination
  and allow all citizens the chance
  to participate freely and actively in forming a state
    and choosing leaders.
Citizens, therefore, have a duty to vote,
  and leaders are to be praised for stepping forth.
A system of law is also a good thing
  when it protects rights
  and furnishes the state with order and support.

But we should be on guard against granting government
    too much authority
    or seeking too much from it,
    because that weakens the sense of responsibility
       on the part of individuals,
          families,
          and groups.
If individual rights are temporarily suspended
    during an emergency,
    they should be restored very quickly.
Citizens, for their part, should be loyal to their country
    but not blind to the needs of the rest of the world.
They should be aware that there will be differences
    about how best to govern
    and enter into the public debate with a good heart.
Those who are suited for it
    should enter the art of politics
    without thought of personal gain
       or benefit of bribery.
Such leaders should oppose
    injustice and oppression,
    oligarchy or arbitrary use of power,
    and intolerance for diversity.

76 We must never confuse the Church
    with the political community
    nor bind it to any political system.
In fact, the political community and the Church
    are mutually independent and self-governing.
The Church's contribution is to introduce love and justice
    into society, not to govern it.
But it is also the Church's legitimate work
    to preach the faith in freedom,
    to teach her social doctrines,

and to discharge her duty among people
    without hindrance.
The Church also has the right to pass moral judgments
    when the salvation of souls is at stake,
    for it is the Church's task to reveal,
        cherish,
        and ennoble
    all that is true,
        good,
        and beautiful
        in the human community.

Chapter Five
THE FOSTERING OF PEACE AND THE
PROMOTION OF A COMMUNITY OF NATIONS

77 "Those who work for peace
    shall be called children of God"
    according to the Gospel of Matthew (5:9),
    and, indeed, in our day, these words
        shed new light on the human family's
        growth toward full development.
For we live in a time of war
    and the threat of war,
    and we are in a great human crisis.
We wish to cooperate with all people of goodwill
    to help establish a solid, lasting peace on earth.

78 Peace, we believe, is not merely the absence of war.
    Nor is it reduced to a silent, cold standoff
        where the parties remain armed.
    And it is not an outcome of dictatorship.

What is it, then?
    Indeed, what is "peace"?

Peace is a harmony built into human society
    by God, the divine Founder of all life,
    and it is a direct outcome of justice.
Such a peace is not attained once and for all
    but is constantly built up
    as people control their passions
        and governments remain vigilant.
But even this is not enough.
    For peace is the fruit of love as well.
It cannot be obtained and safeguarded
    unless men and women freely and trustingly
    share with one another their inner spirits and talents.
It is based on a firm determination to respect others,
    and to live lives of sisterhood and brotherhood.
Without such love, peace absolutely cannot prevail
    in our time.
For all of this flows from the peace of Christ,
    who first loved us
    and dedicated himself for us.
We urge all Christians, therefore,
    to join with all peacemakers in the world
    to plead for peace and bring it about.
We praise those who renounce violence
    and find other ways to settle disputes
    where fairness for all is assured.
We dream of the day when we will say with Isaiah (2:4),
    "They shall beat their swords into plowshares
        and their spears into pruning hooks;
        one nation shall not raise the sword
            against another,
        nor shall they train for war again."

79 Despite this great dream of all people,
    savage warfare goes on all over the world,
    in fact, more savage than ever before.
Having considered all this,
    we in this council remind everyone
    first and foremost
        about the permanent, binding force
        of natural law,
        which is the law written in our very hearts.
Any action that deliberately conflicts with this law
    or any command ordering someone else to do so
        is criminal.
Blind obedience will excuse no one from this.

Among the actions which fall into this category,
    that is, which conflict with natural law,
    is any methodical extermination of an entire people,
        nation,
        or ethnic minority.
No case can be made for such an action!
    It is always horrendously wrong!
Those who oppose such actions
    are highly praised.
International agreements to make military activity
    less inhumane
    should be strengthened and obeyed.

Now, on the subject of war,
    it clearly still exists on earth
    and, therefore, governments cannot be denied
    the right to legitimate defense when attacked;
        indeed, governments have a duty
        to protect their citizens.
But it is one thing to defend oneself or one's nation

and another to move offensively against others.
All who volunteer for armed-service duty
    should think of themselves as agents of peace,
        security,
        and freedom.

80 We undertake an evaluation of war today
    with a new attitude
    because of the presence of weapons
        of total destruction.
Therefore, we hereby condemn total war completely,
    and following the teachings of Pope John XXIII
    in *Pacem in Terris*
    and Pope Paul VI at the United Nations,
        we issue this declaration:
Any act of war aimed indiscriminately at the destruction
    of entire cities
    or of extensive areas
        along with their populations
    is a crime against God and humanity itself
        and merits absolute
        and unhesitating
            condemnation!
What is so unique about this situation
    is that world events might unfold on their own
    in such a way that someone may decide
        to use such a weapon.
In order to help prevent this from happening,
    we bishops of the entire world
    urge all world leaders to consider
    the awesome responsibility that is theirs
        when their nations possess such weapons.
81 We also realize that such weapons,
    based on modern science

and capable of total destruction,
are amassed with the thought in mind
that having them will deter an enemy
from attacking in the first place.
Many regard this as an effective way to keep peace.
We believe, on the contrary,
that this is not a safe way to keep peace at all.
The so-called "balance" that results
is unsure and unsteady,
and the threat of war only increases
as the number of weapons does.
Furthermore, while vast fortunes are spent
to purchase and build these weapons,
the poor continue to starve,
disagreements among nations are not healed,
and the world lives in terrible anxiety.
We say it again: this arms race is a treacherous trap
for all of humanity
and one that injures the poor
to an intolerable degree.
Let us work together to seek another approach,
one more worthy of the dignity of humanity.
If we fail to do this,
we do not know where the evil path
on which we tread
will lead.

82 Peace, then, must be born of mutual trust between nations
rather than a doubtful outcome of their fear
of one another's weapons.
We commit ourselves to work for the day
when war, all war,
can be completely outlawed
by international consent.

In the meantime, let us move toward disarmament,
    not unilaterally but in every nation.
Many world leaders are now working
    to end war,
    and we commend you!
It is time to put aside purely national interests
    so that the whole community of humankind
    can find peace together.

The basis for this is in each person's change of heart
    as we regard the entire world
    and those tasks that we can perform in unison
        for the betterment of all people.
Peace will not come until hatreds end;
    until contempt for others ends;
    until distrust,
        unbending ideologies,
        and divisions
            cease.
The Church now takes its stand in the midst
    of these anxieties,
    which are felt in every nation of the world.
We intend to continually say to all:
    Now is the proper time for change!

83 If peace is indeed to succeed,
    the causes of discord must be reduced,
    especially injustice that results
        from economic inequalities,
        from a quest for power,
        or from contempt for personal rights.

84 The way to do this is for the human family
    sharing this planet together

to create for itself a system of governance
that is sufficient to meet the demands
of these modern times.
We have the beginnings in current international agencies,
and cooperation among all people,
regardless of their religion,
is central to this.
The Church is delighted with the growing
cooperative spirit among nations
both among Christians and non-Christians.

85 These international efforts should also be extended
to the economic field
where wealthy and developed nations
assist others to procure the necessary material goods
for a richer quality of life.
If this is to work, we will have to reduce
excessive desire for profit,
nationalistic pretensions,
the lust for political domination,
militaristic thinking,
and schemes designed to promote ideologies.
86 Toward this end, we can offer some guidelines:
First, as nations develop
they should strongly hold
the complete human fulfillment of their citizens
as the goal of their efforts.
Second, advanced nations have a heavy duty
to assist developing people
toward this end.
Third, the entire world should organize together
to provide for economic growth
but should do so taking into account
the rights of all to determine their own fate

and the duty of all to assist one another.
Fourth, there is a pressing need to reform
    the very structures of economic activity,
    but nations should be wary of solutions
        that nibble away at human spirituality
        or wholeness.

87 We do recognize the need in some places
    to regulate and reduce population growth.
Every effort should be made to distribute food and goods
    more fairly to all
    and, indeed, to increase production when possible.
And since so many people are concerned today
    about controlling population growth,
    we urge that whatever steps are taken
        be in accord with moral law.
The question of how many children a couple should have
    is a matter of conscience
    and not of government-imposed rules.
This parental decision takes into account
    educational and social conditions
    and these modern times.
People should be made aware in a wise manner
    of scientific advances that can help them
    arrange the number of their children.
The reliability of such methods should be proven,
    and they should be in harmony with our ethics.

88 Given all we have said,
    let us add that Christians also have a duty
    to support personally those who are poor.
Certain wealthy nations, with mainly Christian populations,
    must become aware of the deprivation of other nations,
        the torment,

disease,
and hunger in the rest of the world.
Well-organized efforts to share resources
should be undertaken,
ecumenically when possible,
to alleviate suffering everywhere.
As was true in the early years of the Church,
Christians should meet the needs of these poor
out of their own subsistence
and not only from what is "left over."
Collections among Christians should be taken
throughout the entire world
in cooperation, when possible,
with other Christians.

89 The Church stands among the nations
as a catalyst of this activity.
To achieve this, the Church must be present
among the nations
in a thoroughgoing way,
both through her members
as well as institutionally.
90 Toward this end, we at this council
now recommend the establishment of an agency
of the universal Church.
This agency will have the task of promoting justice,
stimulating the Catholic community to participate
and work for social justice
on an international level.
It will take its place among other agencies
and help end the terrible hardships
felt by people around the world today.

Conclusion

91 These proposals, dealing with many modern challenges,
    are meant for all people,
    whether or not they believe in God.
What we have said here is very general
    but it is rooted in the Gospel,
    and we hope further development
        of these ideas
        will produce action.

92 Indeed, the Church itself is a sign of cooperation
    based on honest dialogue.
This requires that we ourselves foster within the Church
    mutual esteem,
    reverence,
    harmony,
    and the full recognition of legitimate diversity.
We embrace those not yet in full communion with us
    to whom we are linked by faith
    and a common bond of charity.
Likewise, we embrace those who do not believe in Christ
    who also await unity and peace.

We fervently wish to have a frank conversation
    with all people of goodwill,
    everyone who seeks goodness and truth,
        excluding no one,
        even those who hate the Church,
        so we can build peace with all.

93 There is nothing, in short,
    for which Christians yearn more
    than to serve the people of the modern world

generously and effectively.
We Christians shoulder a gigantic task
    which is to introduce love into the world,
        that love which we receive ourselves from Christ.
May Christ be with us in our work!

Appendices
and
Index

Appendix One

A Brief Summary of the Documents of Vatican II

Part One: The Four Constitutions

These major documents set direction for the whole Church.

1. Dogmatic Constitution on the CHURCH

(In Latin, *Lumen Gentium.*)

Approved on November 21, 1964, by a vote of 2,151 to 5.

This strong document was argued by the council from the first day to its passage. It was widely supported in the end and set a major new focus for the Church. It treated several key aspects of the Catholic theology of Church.

(1) The Church, this document says, is a mystery, i.e., "a reality imbued with the hidden presence of God." It is a sacrament: a visible, tangible, audible sign of the invisible, intangible, inaudible divinity. (2) The Church, furthermore, is the whole People of God, including but not identical with its hierarchy alone. (3) Bishops, for their part, are to act collegially, together with the pope, the bishop of Rome. (4) By their very vocation, the laity seek the Reign of God by engaging in "temporal" affairs and ordering them according to the plan of God. (5) The call to holiness is a call to

everyone. (6) The consecrated life of women and men religious is a particular gift to the Church. (7) Christians share the Church with those who have died and who now share life with God in heaven. (8) The memory of Mary is to hold a place of reverence for all.

The document contains 69 articles in the following eight chapters:

a. The Mystery of the Church
b. On the People of God
c. On the Hierarchical Structure of the Church and in Particular, on the Episcopate
d. The Laity
e. The Universal Call to Holiness in the Church
f. Religious
g. The Eschatological Nature of the Pilgrim Church and Its Union with the Church in Heaven
h. The Blessed Virgin Mary, Mother of God, in the Mystery of Christ and the Church

2. Dogmatic Constitution on DIVINE REVELATION

(In Latin, *Dei Verbum.*)

Approved on November 18, 1965, by a vote of 2,344 to 6.

This strong document states that the Church moves forward in time, developing an ever deeper understanding of what is handed down about the Reign of God and always finding new ways of expressing that.

The document emphasizes that the Word of God is the foundation of divine revelation, and it corrects the under-standing that there are two equal sources of revelation, namely, tradition and Scripture. It clarifies that the Word of God is found both in sacred tradition as well as in sacred Scripture. God speaks to us, this document explains, in word and deed and calls forth a response from us. We call this response "faith" and through faith we entrust our whole selves to God. This faith is handed on to all generations by *living* traditions. This faith is contained in one sacred deposit, expressed through the teaching office of the Church whose role and duty it is to serve the Word of God.

The document contains 26 articles in the following six chapters:

a. Revelation Itself
b. Handing On Divine Revelation
c. Sacred Scripture: Its Inspiration and Divine Interpretation
d. The Old Testament
e. The New Testament
f. Sacred Scripture in the Life of the Church

3. Constitution on the SACRED LITURGY

(In Latin, *Sacrosanctum Concilium.*)

Approved on December 4, 1963, by a vote of 2,147 to 4.

This constitution has had the most influence in the emergence of the laity after the council because it updates the Mass, including the role of the laity as ministers in the Liturgy, thus bringing about a sea change in Catholic lay self-identity.

The document seeks (1) to give vigor to the Christian life of the faithful, (2) to adapt what is changeable to the needs of today, (3) to promote union among all who believe in Christ, and (4) to strengthen the Church's mission to all humankind. The constitution declares that the Mass (the Liturgy) is the source and summit of the Christian life.

Therefore, for the Liturgy to be effective, the faithful must (1) be well disposed, (2) know what they are doing, and (3) participate. The document established that some things are changeable (language, books, prayers, music, persons, and places) while some are not (Scripture, bread, wine, prayer over the gifts, eucharistic prayer, communion). It also establishes vernacular in worship. The laity cannot participate in Latin. The document restores the Eucharist as an *act* rather than as a *static devotional object*. This means a downplaying of devotions outside of Mass: rosary, benediction, and so on. The lessening of these devotions is felt very strongly by the average Catholic.

Several "instructions" on implementing the document follow it. The first of these instructions was published before the end of the council.

The document contains 130 articles
in the following eight chapters:

a. General Principles for Restoration and
   Promotion of the Sacred Liturgy
b. The Most Sacred Mystery of the Eucharist
c. Other Sacraments and the Sacramentals
d. The Divine Office
e. The Liturgical Year
f. Sacred Music
g. Sacred Art and Furnishings
h. Appendix: A Declaration of the Second Vatican
   Council on the Revision of the Calendar

4. Pastoral Constitution on the
CHURCH IN THE MODERN WORLD

(In Latin, *Gaudium et Spes*.)

Approved on December 7, 1965, by a vote of 2,309 to 75.

This important historic document speaks to the Church and to all people about the hopes and dreams of the human family. It is the first document issued by such a council to address the whole world.

"The joy and hope, the grief and anxiety of the people of this age, especially those who are poor or in any way afflicted, this is the joy and hope, the grief and anxiety of the followers of Christ." Modern Christians must look at and trust the signs of the times and understand the world in which they live. (Contrast this with Pius IX's *Syllabus of Errors* in 1864, which says that the pope "cannot and should not be reconciled and come to terms with progress, liberalism, and modern civilization.")

The human person is dignified but many still suffer. Human "conscience is the most secret core and sanctuary of a person where he or she is alone with God." But there is a mysterious aspect to human nature, and conscience is not easily discerned. Modern people live together in a global community of persons for which there must be made available everything necessary for leading a truly human life. Every type of discrimination is to be overcome and eradicated as contrary to God's intent. Science does not conflict with faith.

The Church lives and acts in the world. "Let there be no false opposition between professional and social activities on the one part, and religious life on the other." It is not "the world against the Church." It is "the world together with the Church."

The document contains 93 articles
in the following nine chapters:

a.   The Dignity of the Human Person
b.   The Community of Humankind
c.   Humans' Activity throughout the World
d.   The Role of the Church in the Modern World
e.   Fostering the Nobility of Marriage and the
     Family
f.   The Proper Development of Culture
g.   Economic and Social Life
h.   The Life of the Political Community
i.   The Fostering of Peace and the Promotion of a
     Community of Nations

PART TWO: THE NINE DECREES

These are significant documents, to be used in further reflection. They set a pace and direction for further discussion.

1. Decree on the Instruments of SOCIAL COMMUNICATION

(In Latin, *Inter Mirifica*.)

Approved on December 4, 1963, by a vote of 1,960 to 164.

This relatively weak document is condescending in tone and is addressed to the media and those who control it. The document calls for the Church to use modern media to preach the Gospel. It also calls for the faithful to reject what is ungodly in the media. The document is seen by most theologians as out of touch with the overall theology of the council. It was one of the first to be passed.

The document contains 24 articles
in the following two chapters:

a. On the Teaching of the Church
b. On the Pastoral Activity of the Church

2. Decree on ECUMENISM

(In Latin, *Unitatis Redintegratio.*)

Approved on November 21, 1964, by a vote of 2,137 to 11.

This document represents a major move forward for the Church. It seeks restoration of ties with other Christians rather than their return to Rome. The document admits that blame for separation exists on both sides and calls for a change of heart to make ecumenism possible. Eucharistic sharing may at times be necessary for the gaining of the grace of unity (n. 8). The document encourages dialogue and calls for the Roman Church to reform itself as part of the process of reunion.

The document contains 24 articles
in the following three chapters:

a. Catholic Principles on Ecumenism
b. The Practice of Ecumenism
c. Churches and Ecclesial Communities Separated from the Roman Apostolic See

3. Decree on the EASTERN CATHOLIC CHURCHES

(In Latin, *Orientalium Ecclesiarum.*)

Approved on November 21, 1964, by a vote of 2,110 to 39.

This minor document gives Rome's perspective on the six main Eastern Rite Churches: Chaldean, Syrian, Maronite, Coptic, Armenian, and Byzantine. It states an ardent desire for reconciliation and clearly proclaims the equality of the Eastern and Western traditions.

The document contains 30 articles
in the following six chapters:

a.   The Individual Churches or Rites
b.   Preservation of the Spiritual Heritage of the
      Eastern Churches
c.   Eastern Rite Patriarchs
d.   The Disciplines of the Sacraments
e.   Divine Worship
f.   Relations with the Brethren of the Separated
      Churches

4. Decree on the BISHOPS' PASTORAL OFFICE in the Church

(In Latin, *Christus Dominus.*)

Approved on October 28, 1965, by a vote of 2,319 to 2.

This is a follow-up document to the one on the Church. It gives a job description for bishops and stresses the need for shared decision making (collegiality). The document also calls for bishops to be servant leaders and establishes diocesan pastoral councils.

The document contains 44 articles
in the following four chapters:

a. The Relationship of Bishops to the Universal Church
b. Bishops and Their Particular Churches or Dioceses
c. Concerning Bishops Cooperating for the Common Good of Many Churches
d. General Directive

5. Decree on PRIESTLY FORMATION

(In Latin, *Optatam Totius.*)

Approved on October 28, 1965, by a vote of 2,318 to 3.

This document revises the rules for seminary training which had been established at the Council of Trent 450 years earlier. It calls for training in Scripture, pastoral counseling, ecumenism, history, and personal formation. The document also allows for local training guidelines to produce priests more ready to deal with local pastoral realities.

The document contains 22 articles
in the following seven chapters:

a. The Program of Priestly Training to Be Undertaken by Each Country
b. The Urgent Fostering of Priestly Vocations
c. The Setting Up of Major Seminaries
d. The Careful Development of the Spiritual Training
e. The Revision of Ecclesiastical Studies

f. The Promotion of Strictly Pastoral Training
g. Training to Be Achieved after the Course of Studies

6. Decree on the APPROPRIATE RENEWAL OF RELIGIOUS LIFE

(In Latin, *Perfectae Caritatis.*)

Approved on October 28, 1965, by a vote of 2,321 to 4.

This document urges religious women and men (1) to return to their roots, that is, their reasons for being founded and (2) to adjust to the needs of changing times in the modern Church. It does not repeat the teaching of Trent that religious life is a superior state to that of the married.

The document contains 25 articles all in one chapter.

7. Decree on the APOSTOLATE OF THE LAITY

(In Latin, *Apostolicam Actuositatem.*)

Approved on November 18, 1965, by a vote of 2,305 to 2.

Although this document has less influence than the constitutions, it is important as the first document in the history of ecumenical councils to address itself to anyone other than the Church's own clergy. The document declares that by virtue of their baptisms, the laity have a ministry, not merely a sharing in the ministry of the ordained. This lengthy document details how the apostolic work of the laity is to proceed and how laypersons are to be prepared for this work.

It also places great emphasis on the importance of each person's role in the establishment of the Reign of God.

The document contains 33 articles
in the following seven chapters:

a. The Vocation of the Laity to the Apostolate
b. Objectives
c. The Various Fields of the Apostolate
d. The Various Forms of the Apostolate
e. External Relationships
f. Formation for the Apostolate
g. Exhortation

8. Decree on the MINISTRY AND LIFE OF PRIESTS

(In Latin, *Presbyterorum Ordinis.*)

Approved on December 7, 1965, by a vote of 2,390 to 4.

This last-minute document does not address the social needs of today's priests. (A later synod in 1970 tried to make up for this weakness.) It calls on priests to support the laity and reaffirms celibacy for priests of the Latin Rite. The document says that, although it is not demanded by the very nature of the priesthood, celibacy seems "suitable."

The document contains 22 articles
in the following four chapters:

a. The Priesthood in the Mission of the Church
b. The Ministry of Priests
c. The Life of Priests
d. Conclusion and Exhortation

9. Decree on the Church's MISSIONARY ACTIVITY

(In Latin, *Ad Gentes.*)

Approved on December 7, 1965, by a vote of 2,394 to 5.

This document encourages retaining local religious customs and incorporating the Gospel into them, a radical idea. It also states that the whole Church is missionary, meaning that all the People of God are called to introduce others to the faith. The document tries to consolidate all the strains of ecclesiology discussed elsewhere.

The document contains 41 articles
in the following six chapters:

a. Doctrinal Principles
b. Mission Work Itself
c. Particular Churches
d. Missionaries
e. Planning Missionary Activity
f. Cooperation

PART THREE: THE THREE DECLARATIONS

These statements of theological position are important for their influence on future dialogue.

1. Declaration on CHRISTIAN EDUCATION

(In Latin, *Gravissimum Educationis.*)

Approved on October 28, 1965, by a vote of 2,290 to 35.

This weak document leaves most of the work to postconciliar development. It is still under study today.

The document contains 12 articles on these topics:

a. The Meaning of the Universal Right to an Education
b. Christian Education
c. The Authors of Education
d. Various Aids to Christian Education
e. The Importance of Schools
f. The Duties and Rights of Parents
g. Moral and Religious Education in All Schools
h. Catholic Schools
i. Different Types of Catholic Schools
j. Catholic Colleges and Universities
k. Coordination to Be Fostered in Scholastic Matters

2. Declaration on the RELATIONSHIP OF THE CHURCH TO NON-CHRISTIANS

(In Latin, *Nostra Aetate*.)

Approved on October 28, 1965, by a vote of 2,221 to 88.

This earthshaking document began as a statement only about the Church's relations with the Jews but was widened to say that the "truth" is present outside the Body of Christ and is to be respected wherever it is found, mentioning in particular Hinduism, Buddhism, and Islam, as well as Judaism. The Catholic Church, it states, encourages dialogue and opens itself to the contributions of these others. Most importantly, the document states that God loves the Jews and that they cannot be blamed as a race for the death of Jesus. The document condemns every form of persecution or discrimination against the Jews.

The document contains five articles all in one chapter.

3. Declaration on RELIGIOUS FREEDOM

(In Latin, *Dignitatis Humanae*.)

Approved on December 7, 1965, by a vote of 2,308 to 70.

This most controversial of council documents began as a chapter in the document on ecumenism. The document allows for the development of doctrine and says that the freedom of persons requires that no one ever be forced to join the Church. The Church claims freedom for itself in this document, but also for all religious practice of every kind everywhere.

The document contains 15 articles all in one chapter.

Appendix Two

A Carefully Annotated Reading List on Vatican II

PART ONE: THE DOCUMENTS

The Documents of Vatican II
Walter M. Abbott, S.J.

Most of the standard writings on the council will use this translation. (Costello Publishing Company, 1975, 1984.)

Vatican Council II
Austin Flannery, O.P.

This is good for postconciliar documents and statements. Also, a second volume shows how the council's decisions are being implemented. (Scholarly Resources, 1975; William B. Eerdmans, New Revised Edition, 1988.)

Decrees of the Ecumenical Councils (two volumes)
ed. Norman P. Tanner, S.J.

This reference book provides English translations of all the documents of each ecumenical council in the entire history of the Church. It has excellent indices. (Sheed & Ward, 1990; Georgetown University Press, 1990.)

PART TWO: GENERAL WORKS
ON THE COUNCIL

Destination: Vatican II
Thomas More

This highly interactive and detailed CD-ROM includes all major works on Vatican II including Walter Abbott's edition of the documents, the Daybooks, Xavier Rynne, Bill Huebsch's paraphrase text, timelines, biographies, interviews, and much more! (Thomas More Publishing, 1996.)

The Faithful Revolution: Vatican II
Thomas More

This five part video documentary was derived from more than 170 hours of live interviews with many of the council's participants and observers. It tells the story of Vatican II's legacy in an unbiased and complete fashion. (Thomas More Publishing, 1996.)

The Second Vatican Council and the New Catholicism
G. Berkouwer

Berkouwer was an observer at the council, and he has some interesting observations from a non-Catholic point of view. (William B. Eerdmans, 1965.)

The Theology of Vatican II
Dom Christopher Butler

The excellent introduction to this book gives very helpful background for both Vatican I and Vatican II. The work itself is also excellent, but not for beginners. (Darton, Longman & Todd, 1967; Christian Classics, 1981.)

The Joannine Council
Bernard Häring

Häring was one of the liberal *periti* at Vatican II. He pioneered a whole new approach to moral theology. (Herder and Herder, 1963.)

The Council Reform and Reunion
Hans Küng

This work made Küng a household name. He presents the problems and expectations for the council on the eve of Vatican II. The sale of this book in Rome was banned during the first session of the council. (Sheed & Ward, 1961.)

Vatican Council II
Xavier Rynne

This is a detailed account of the proceedings of the council itself and is still the best for accuracy, style, and astute observation. This version is a condensed edition of Rynne's four volumes, one for each session. (Farrar, Straus and Giroux, 1968.)

A Spirituality of Wholeness: The New Look at Grace
Bill Huebsch

This book offers a treatment of the theology of grace which formed the basis of the work done at the council. It is written in easy-to-read sense lines and common English. (Twenty-Third Publications, 1994.)

Rethinking Sacraments: Holy Moments in Daily Living
Bill Huebsch

Another book by the same author in the same style, this volume details the shift in focus which the council enacted in its reform of the traditional seven sacraments of the Church. (Twenty-Third Publications, 1993.)

American Participation in the Second Vatican Council
Vincent Yzermans

This book is a very complete compilation of speeches and other contributions made by U.S. prelates and *periti* during Vatican II. Its index is outstanding. (Sheed & Ward, 1967.)

Vatican II: An Interfaith Appraisal
Edited by John Miller

Miller edited an excellent group of articles, including many that tell the story of the actual debates at the council. To really gain an insight into how the reforms unfolded, read this. The book is out of print but available in used book stores. (Universary of Notre Dame Press and Association Press, 1966.)

A Man Called John
Alden Hatch

No study of the council is complete without reading a biography of John XXIII. This one is brief, readable, and objective. (Hawthorne Books, 1963.)

A Concise History of the Catholic Church
Thomas Bokenkotter

This classic should be on everyone's bookshelf. There is simply no better, more objective postconciliar history of the Church for readability and indexing. (Doubleday, 1977.)

The Church Emerging from Vatican II
Dennis M. Doyle

This is a very well written and easy-to-read treatment of how the council affected the day-to-day life of the Church. Doyle is a scholar on the council and his book makes wide use of anecdotes and stories as a way of situating the council in today's Church. (Twenty-Third Publications, 1994.)

Council Daybook (three volumes)
Edited by Floyd Anderson

For the most complete story of the council's proceedings from the opening speeches to the closing bell, read this. It can be easily browsed and has a very detailed index if one is looking for something specific. It is only available in used book stores. (National Council Welfare Conference, [1962–63] 1965, [1964] 1965, [1965] 1966.)

Council Speeches of Vatican II
Yves Congar, Hans Küng, and Daniel O'Hanlon

Selected by three leading *periti*, these speeches are also included in the daybooks. But this small volume is more available and easier to hold than they are. (Sheed & Ward, 1964.)

Catholicism
Richard McBrien

It goes without saying that this is a handbook for every Catholic, and it presents the outcomes of Vatican II very faithfully. Everyone should own this book. To make it more affordable, McBrien's book is available in softcover editions. (Winston Press, 1981.)

The Catechism of the Catholic Church

This official, comprehensive treatment of the Catholic faith includes an excellent index which gives generous attention to the impact that Vatican II has had on the modern Church. (Harper San Francisco, 1994.)

Index

Book Two: The Four Constitutions

Book Three: The Decrees and Declarations

BILL HUEBSCH

Topic	Document	Article
• call to participate in ecumenical activity	Ecumenism	4
• joining in prayer with others	Ecumenism	8
• understanding theology of others	Ecumenism	9
• great movement toward ecumenism	Ecumenism	1
• defined	Ecumenism	4
• need for new members to nourish openness	Missionary Activity	15
• need for education and theology	Ecumenism	10

Laity

• laypeople working for the Church	Laity	22
• place of laypeople in their cultures	Laity	29
• Church not able to function without laypeople	Laity	1
• role to play in life and activity of Church	Laity	10
• ordinary lay life as holy	Church	34
• secular duties belong to laypeople	Modern World	43
• apostolate of laypeople	Laity	esp. 1–2, 6, 13–14, 20, 23–25
also:	Communications	16
	Church	13, 35
	Bishops	17, 30

TOPIC	DOCUMENT	ARTICLE
• educational systems must allow freedom	Education	7
• the right to needs and freedoms	Modern World	26
• freedom of religion is for all	Modern World	73, 76
• definition of religious freedom	Religious Liberty	2
• role of government in assuring freedom	Religious Liberty	6
• false religious freedom abuses people	Religious Liberty	7
• roots in revelation of freedom	Religious Liberty	9
• no one is to be forced to join the Church	Missionary Activity	13
• the Church's own freedoms insured	Modern World	42
also:	Bishops	20
	Religious Liberty	13

RENEWAL OF RELIGIOUS LIFE

• men and women religious should be properly trained	Religious Life	18
• renewal of religious life rooted in founders	Religious Life	1–2
• sisters should be equal	Religious Life	15
• vocations should be encouraged	Religious Life	24
• religious and laity harmonize ministry	Laity	23
• testimony of religious to world	Church	31, 46
also:	Religious Life	12, 24

Topic	Document	Article
• the specific curial office governing the spread of the Faith	Missionary Activity	29

NATURE OF MARRIAGE

• sacred nature of marriage and its place in life	Modern World	47–52
• married life as place where Christ dwells	Church	35
• marriage as an apostolate of the laity	Laity	11
• decision on number of children belongs to couple	Modern World	87
also:	Church	51
• spouses lead each other to holiness	Church	11, 41
• rights of parents defined	Laity	11
also:	Education	7–8

BAPTISM

• baptism into one Body	Church	7
• baptism and marriage	Church	11
• necessity of baptism	Church	14
• baptism and Paschal Mystery	Liturgy	6
• as the basis for unity	Ecumenism	3, 22
• a holy priesthood of baptized	Church	10
• the call to unity	Missionary Activity	6